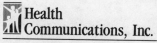

MAKING FRIENDS

Leaving Loneliness Behind

Men And Women Can Be Friends

Perry Treadwell, Ph.D.

Health Communications, Inc.
Deerfield Beach, Florida

Library of Congress Cataloging-in-Publication Data

Treadwell, Perry
    Making friends, leaving loneliness behind: men and women can be
friends / Perry Treadwell.
      p.   cm.
    Includes bibliographical references.
    ISBN 1-55874-227-1
    1. Friendship. 2. Loneliness. 3. Men-women relationships. 4. Sex
differences (Psychology) I. Title.
BF575.F66T74   1992   92-22547
158'.2—dc20   CIP

©1993 Perry Treadwell
ISBN 1-55874-227-1

Publisher: Health Communications, Inc.
            3201 S.W. 15th Street
            Deerfield Beach, Florida 33442-8190

Cover design by Iris T. Slones

Dedication

Dedicated to my children,
Gilbert, Gail, Sally and Susan,
and my grandchildren,
Sarah, Amanda and Amy

Acknowledgments

I am indebted to many people who stimulated my curiosity and supported my constant probing. Those unnamed people who opened up their lonely, sometimes addicted, lives to me are the heroes of this book. They have been my guides to discovery and understanding.

The Emory University Library provided excellent resource service. Kirk Elifson of Georgia State University helped with the loneliness questionnaire. Carl Bronn, in helping me with my statistics, focused me on important questions. Myra Gross improved my words without losing my voice. Barbara Nichols of Health Communications has been a friendly editor which, she has taught me, is not an oxymoron.

I thank my friend, Ted Davis, for his constancy in the ups and downs of this labor of love. For in the end that is what this book is all about: learning to love one another. That is what friends are for. In the end that is all there really is to our short visit on this planet.

Drop everything. Learn to be a friend.

Perry Treadwell
Decatur, Georgia

Contents

Preface

*My tender and golden love, you were my
other loneliness, the only clasp of hand and heart
that I had. I was a stranger, alone and lost in the
wilderness, and I found you. We were forsaken and lost,
as all men are in ninety countries among the
eighteen million people of this earth.
My dear, my darling, we were the only
lights in that enormous dark.*

Thomas Wolfe, August 1928

Friendship is the glue that holds society together. In spite of social earthquakes shaking our communities and families apart, friends and families make life worth living. It often takes a real effort to maintain well-balanced personal relationships. But if we cannot be responsible participants in intimate relationships with families and friends, how can we possibly expect to foster friendships between the larger families or nations of our global village? And if we fail, will the human race be fated to extinction like the dinosaurs on this earth?

It's Time We Took Time

My experience leading workshops on *Making Friendships* assures me that we are capable of making and maintaining friends. Yet we are too distracted, too busy and just plain rusty in our friendship skills to take the time to make friends. Often in the past, sexual involvement distorted the possibilities of forming friendships. But in this age of AIDS and a whole dictionary of other sexually transmitted diseases, we had better learn some more stable ways of satisfying our needs for close affiliation with others.

This is an opportune time for men and women to declare a truce in "The Longest War" and discover the fruits of friendship which only equality can bring.

It is all too common in sexual relationships for one participant to have more power than the other, but true friendship demands equality.

Once the suggestion, some would call it the *obligation*, of sexual intercourse is held in abeyance, friendships between the sexes opens up an entirely new dimension of interactions.

This is what my workshops, and this book, are about.

Friendship Workshops

The fun of doing my workshops year after year is to watch the participants discover that men and women *can* be friends — once the specter of sex is dissolved. Even if friendship does develop into a more intimate, sexual relationship, a firm foundation of autonomy based on communication has already been established.

Origins

In 1977 a small men's support group which I formed was turned into the larger *The Men's Experience* by myself and others. It was a safe place for men to come together to explore their own fears and foibles. I soon learned that men hunger for the friendship of other men but don't know how to make and nurture these friendships. During the '80s I developed workshops for men on making friends. When I offered this workshop to the public, it wasn't long before women began showing up. I adjusted the workshop for both sexes. These sessions helped men and women discover what they want in friendships, what barriers they erect and how to nurture the friendships they had and develop new ones.

Coping With Our Loneliness

Once I started asking questions about loneliness, I began to understand why my earlier attempts at changing the world were so fruitless. The security of belonging can blind people to the need for change. For example, people were joining the local environmental group, formed to promote conservation and reduce consumption, for the social stroking and the group identity — and not to do the hard work needed to change people's attitudes. I found that people were joining the peace movement to "get laid." Marching and civil disobedience are scary; the assurance of a warm body makes the dark a little safer.

What is new is the perspective that men and women belong to slightly different cultures. Learning to communicate between the cultures holds the promise of creating a new level of human relationships.

What is new about defining loneliness is its association with our childhood experience. Phillip Shaver and his colleagues have been studying the association of loneliness with childhood attachment experiences. The ghosts of childhood continue to haunt us. This book is intended to help readers discover the origins of those ghosts so that they can be exorcised. Good hunting.

What is new is the realization that loneliness is not an emotion to be avoided, but a symptom of unattachment to be treated with creative activities either alone or with friends.

What is new is the recent discoveries of the relationship between the feelings of attachment, of belonging, and the chemicals in our bodies which transmit these feelings. I draw on my experience as a biologist and my training at the U.C.L.A. Brain Research Institutes to make these connections.

What is new is observing the connection between the behaviors we use to numb our loneliness and addictions. Frequently it seems easier to treat our loneliness with overwork, overeating, drugs and alcohol or instant sex rather than seek out and develop healthy friendships.

What is also new and most exciting is the growing number of groups designed to put us in touch with ourselves and with one another. These range from therapy and 12-Step programs to men's or women's support groups. Continuing education classes in self-improvement or self-discovery may also fill some needs. Whatever the format, a safe place is created where people can communicate their fears and discover that they are not the only ones to experience the emotions associated with loneliness.

In my workshops, people are discovering that the barriers they have raised to friendships are common and can be removed or overcome.

CHAPTER · ONE

What Is Friendship?

———— * ————

*Friendship is a heart-flooding feeling
that can happen to any two people who are
caught up in the act of being themselves,
together, and who like what they see.
The feeling is deeper than companionship;
one can hire a companion. It is more than
affection; affection can be as false as a stage kiss.
It is never one sided. It elevates biology into
full humanity. Friendship. We know it when
we feel it but we can spend years
trying to put it into words.*

— Letty Pogrebin, *Among Friends*

What is friendship? Ask a man that question and you'll have one set of answers. Ask a woman the same question and you'll have an entirely different set of answers.

If men and women define the word "friendship" differently, by what measure can they judge the quality of friendship between individuals of the opposite sex? If men's and women's expectations of friendship are different, are they bound to be disappointed? Are relationships between men and women even possible without sexual overtones? Is it possible for men and women to be in love and to be "best friends" with their lover or spouse?

These are only a few of the many questions that have been explored in my *Making Friendships* workshops over the past two decades. But we must have a starting point. Our first challenge is to overcome the hurdle of language. We have to learn to communicate clearly.

Is there a universal understanding of the word "friendship" that transcends gender?

Expressing the feelings of friendship in words has never been easy. One of the most articulate individuals of this century and the long-time host of Public Television's *Masterpiece Theater*, Alistair Cooke, has written a book about six of his famous friends and attempts to define friendship:

> What is involved in such relationships is a form of emotional chemistry, so far unexplained by any school of psychiatry I am aware of, that conditions nothing so simple as a choice between

3

two poles of attraction and repulsion. You can meet some people thirty, forty times down the years, and they remain amiable bystanders, like the shore lights of towns that a sailor passes at stated times but never calls at on the regular run. Conversely, all considerations of sex aside, you can meet some other people once or twice and they remain permanent influences on your life.

It is the ineffable, the mystical, the indescribable which makes definition of friendship difficult. Contemporary society uses the term "friend" as indiscriminately as "love." When a person identifies another as a "friend," a whole spectrum of relationships comes to mind.

Letty Pogrebin lists some of these as acquaintances, neighbors, confederates, pals, close kin, co-workers and, finally, friends.

Friendship is a relationship, but it is also an emotion.

What Does Friendship Do For Us?

Friends act as mirrors to our lives. From our very first childhood playmates to adult intimates, friends tell us who we are and also how we *should* behave in our culture. Friends keep us floating above the lonely depths of isolation. The more our busy lives isolate us, the more we need friends to put us back together.

C.S. Lewis, the author of children's stories, science fiction and religious essays, tells us that friendship is one of the four loves; the others are affection, Eros and charity. He says:

> [Friendship], free from instinct, free from all duties but those which love has freely assumed, almost wholly free from jealousy, and free without qualification from the need to be needed, is eminently spiritual.

Here confusion sneaks in, clouding the distinction between caring *for* rather than caring *about*. Most all of us have been trapped into taking care of some needy person and believing that this was friendship. In defining friendship we must learn to discern the difference between a friend who needs us temporarily and a needy person.

If making friendships appeared easy in childhood, for many of us it became more and more difficult through adolescence and adulthood. Making friendships takes effort and attention. But the alternative is to continue our stressed and lonely lives. Friendship promises a more exciting and healthier life.

Some people dream of sexual relationships that will fix everything. But in reality, they may only cause more confusion.

Other people realize they need touching, not sex.

Still others find their only "family" is their friends at work. And when they go home, they go home to a bottle of booze or a rented movie and a pint of ice cream. For these people, loneliness has become a habit that is relatively more comfortable than risking attachment.

It took some time for me to discover that those who attended my *Making Friendships* workshops were lonely. From 18 to 81, they were seeking ways of belonging. This led me to an intense examination of loneliness and human attachment needs. People need people. The need for human attachment doesn't disappear after childhood. What changes is how that need is ultimately satisfied.

Our lives are driven by two insatiable hungers, opposite poles that are pulling us apart. *We need to belong.* We hunger for the feeling of attachment to others. Yet we seek escape from these intimates to feel autonomous. We discover our sense of self by trying to balance affiliation with autonomy. Today we are out of balance as individuals and as a society — a society of isolates longing for satisfying connections.

The Lonely Crowd

The old connections are fragmenting. Families divide and fuse like a culture of protozoa. Neighborhoods disintegrate. The workplace alienates. Schools attempt to manufacture living robots for the wide maw of industry. People we choose to be our heroes have faltered and failed. As our human attachments deteriorate, we attempt to belong by emphasizing our ethnic identity.

Some search for guides in metaphysics, in crystals and tarot cards, just as our grandparents used Ouija boards and séances.

Labeling Americans as lonely is not new. In 1950 David Riesman and his colleagues called their study of "the changing American character" *The Lonely Crowd.* In 1962 Dell published a collection of

writings about "alienation in modern society" called *Man Alone.*
Philip Slater subtitled *The Pursuit of Loneliness* "American Culture at
the Breaking Point" in 1970. Several other popular books on the
loneliness of American society have been published since then.
Academics have also been active researchers in the field following
Richard Weiss's *Loneliness: The Experience of Emotional and Social Isolation.* Such interest can be traced back to the eminent psychiatrist
Gregory Zilboorg's 1938 article, "Loneliness," in *The Atlantic Monthly.* He identified temporary loneliness as the absence of a loved
one. A more profound hopelessness he called the "narcissistically
lonely." His candidates for this loneliness included Wagner,
Nietzsche, Tchaikovsky, Tolstoy, Baudelaire and Dostoyevsky.

You don't need to be a scholar to discover our national loneliness. Just listen to our music. The thread of loneliness runs
through every decade. It is best represented in the national vernacular of Blues and Country and Western. The late Roy Orbison
made his reputation around loneliness with "Only the Lonely"
(1960). Hurtin' and flirtin' was Hank William's trademark.

In the 1920s, she was "All Alone" by the telephone. The '30s
began with "Mood Indigo," while Frank Sinatra lamented that
"Saturday Night Is the Loneliest Night of the Week" in the '40s.
Elvis Presley crooned "Are You Lonesome Tonight?" in 1960, and
the Beatles wondered where all the lonely people came from in
"Eleanor Rigby."

The pain of not belonging has been whining out over our
airwaves hourly and hasn't stopped yet.

Does loneliness always mean a desire for a romantic or sexual
relationship as many of these songs imply? Or can our need for
human attachments be satisfied through the development of
friendships?

The key issue here is that many emotions associated with
friendship are often confused with sexual feelings. Many of our
expectations about sexual partnerships are imposed upon the
love we expect from friends.

C.S. Lewis observed:

> [We] can have erotic love and friendship for the same person, yet
> in some ways nothing is less like a friendship than a love affair.
> Lovers are always talking to one another about their love; friends

hardly ever about their friendship. Lovers are normally face to face, absorbed in each other; friends, side by side, absorbed in some common interest.

Not knowing the difference between the lover and the friend has made friendships between men and women difficult. The confusion is exacerbated by the differences between men's friendships with other men and women's friendships with other women. When asked, we can put words and descriptions to friendship. However, these words have different meanings and men and women have different expectations. These differences are added to the differences resulting from our separate growing-up experiences.

Men expect comradeship; women expect connection.

Men's Expectations

Comradeship is usually built on a shared experience, an adversity or a triumph. It is evident in the yells and hugs seen in locker rooms of winning teams; it is the arm around the shoulder in consolation; it is joshing, storytelling at the local tavern; it is camouflage-uniformed men hugging and crying in front of the Vietnam Memorial; it is a willingness to drop everything to help a buddy; it is a memory of a warm feeling of friends hanging out together with all the armor shed; it is the knowledge that one person is "there" if needed. It is all of the above and yet none are sufficient to call it bonding. For it contains a mystical union only understood by those who have felt it — so easily formed in childhood, so difficult to find in adulthood.

Women's Expectations

Women's friendships are, unlike men's, highly verbal. Friendship is the whispered pain and sadness; the cry of joy. It is the excited conversation spiced with bursts of laughter as women huddle around the restaurant table; the long-distance telephone call on Sunday night when you can talk for hours. It is the expression of emotions accompanied by sudden tears; it is unexpected cards and letters, birthdays remembered, small gifts and flowers. Above all, it is a sense of community built with years of intimate conversations as well as rising from a group success — a win.

Melding The Two

What has kept men and women from being friends? Until recently it was a matter of perceived inequality. Inequality and cultural differences made sexual intercourse the only intimate communication possible between genders.

Equality is the basis of all friendships. Until men and women can regard themselves and each other as equals, no friendship is possible. There are a few examples of documented friendships in the past, between men and women of high social class or sophistication, such as Lady Diana Cooper with author Evelyn Waugh; and salonist Madame d'Epinay with Jean-Jacques Rousseau and diplomat Abbé Galiani.

Next, the cultural differences between the sexes must be recognized. We need to talk about and understand the differences in the early socialization of boys and girls that produce men and women with profound cultural orientations.

The famous friends noted above exchanged written clarifications about what they wanted from their friendship and what kind of friends they would be. Rousseau, after describing the grief a friend's wrong can give him, says to d'Epinay: "But, my dear friend, let us speak frankly; do you know any friends that I have? On my honour, it has been my good fortune to learn to do without them . . . Do not therefore be surprised if my hatred for Paris increases. I get nothing from it but annoyance, with the exception of your letters. . . ."

Finally sex, the ghost at the banquet between cross-sex friends, must be exorcised. Sexual intercourse turns a friendship upside-down. Like Macbeth railing at Banquo's ghost, we will go mad if we don't agree on the sexual ground rules.

So the opportunity for cross-sex friendship is new. We can write our own scenarios. I like novelist Rita Mae Brown's view of her male friendships:

> My best friend, Bill, identifies with my career. If I take a beating
> on a book, Bill is right by my side. He's on my team. He'll threaten

to punch out a critic or he'll say, "Come on, let's ride up in the Blue Ridge and forget these turkeys."

Her male friends do things with her while they talk. She says, "I need my men friends. I learn something from them that I can't learn from women, namely, what it is like to be a man."

A Working Definition

If we are looking for a perfect friendship, we will not find one. There is no perfect definition either. A good start in the search for a workable definition comes from *Loving and Living* by Gerald Phillips and Lloyd Goodall. A friend is described as:

> A person with whom one has had long-term contact (two years or more for starters), involving sharing of intimate information, exchange of mutual support and continuing interaction usually involving at least one serious test where a sacrifice to sustain the relationship was required.

What Do You Expect?

What do you expect in a friendship? After the attendees at their first workshop have identified themselves and why they have risked coming to my workshop on *Making Friendships*, they are asked that question. Here is how to ask yourself. Think about your best friend or friends past or present.

- What made that friendship special?
- What do you expect from such a friendship?
- Are these expectations different for a cross-sex rather than a same-sex friendship?

Our workshop attendees brainstormed 64 expectations before they began to repeat themselves. The first dozen were:

availability	listening	warmth
honesty	presence	spontaneity
trust	fun	support
acceptance	loyalty	vulnerability

Some of the words may have had special meaning for those who offered them. Others are common to many of us. The list is

overwhelming and overlapping. We can boil it down to something
more manageable.

Look at the words used by six people who have written books
or articles about friendship (Table 1-1 on the following page).
When Stuart Miller discovered he did not have any friends following a divorce, he drew up some criteria for friendship:

commitment	complicity	engagement
intimacy	courage	acceptance
relaxation		

Compare these words to those used by the five other authors
identified in Table 1.1. Drury Sherrod and Keith Davis are two
male scholars. Two popular female authors, Lillian Rubin and Letty
Pogrebin, have written books on friendship; and Harold Lyon, a
West Point graduate, also described his search for friendship.

Notice how the nomenclature of friendship is interactive. We
won't try to squeeze the criteria used by the other authors into
Miller's seven words. "Understanding" cited by Rubin and Davis
and "empathy" identified by Lyon might be related to intimacy.
The words used in Table 1.1 build on and define one another and
help us to clarify our values.

To be so methodical and analytical about something as ephem-
eral, enigmatic and romanticized as friendship could seem to some
a sacrilege, to others an insult or even a fruitless exercise. Yet
love, sex and marriage have been dissected much more extensive-
ly. And friendship is an important part of all three.

Think about these words describing friendship. What does each
mean to you?

Table 1.1. Some Nomenclature Of Friendship

Miller	Sherrod	Rubin	Davis	Pogrebin	Lyon
Commitment	Commitment	Commitment Loyalty		Loyalty	Commitment Loyalty
Intimacy		Understanding	Understanding	Intimacy	Empathy
Relaxation		Respect Mutuality	Respect	Similarity	Vulnerability
Courage		Trust Safety Honesty	Trust	Trust Honesty	Trust Realness Genuineness
Engagement	Companionship	Constancy	Enjoyment	Reciprocal Liking	Prizing
Complicity	Sensual active association	Generosity Support	Mutual assistance	Generosity	Equality in nourishing
Acceptance	Acceptance	Acceptance	Acceptance	Acceptance	Accepting

What Do You Want?

Before going any further, take a few moments to rank your expectations of friendship by rating the importance of the characteristics listed below.

Instructions: On a scale of 1 to 7 rate how important each of the following characteristics is in each of the relationships. A score of 1 means the item is *never* or *almost never* important. A score of 7 means that it is *always* or *almost always* important.

What you want in a friendship with a Friend of the	Same Sex	Other Sex	Significant Partner
Commitment (Loyalty) — to be there when I need him/her no matter what	3		7
Intimacy — willingness to share feelings and details about self	5		4
Relaxation — easy to hang out with	5		5
Courage (Trust, Honesty) — willing to challenge me	5		5
Engagement — frequently thinks of me, calls or writes	4		7
Complicity — we have our own ways of doing things together	5		6
Acceptance — no matter how "weird" I am at times I am still okay	5		6

What Do Others Want?

Members of my *Making Friendships* workshops have come from fairly diverse communities, but they share a common interest in discovering what friendship is all about. Some of the participants did not like ranking their expectations at all. Others found the words were ambiguous and could be defined differently. What was your experience?

Making Friendships Workshops

I came to lead the workshops on *Making Friendships* after discovering that men have a difficult time making friends. I was part of a large men's support group at the time and heard men say that their best friend was back in college, the military or hundreds of miles away. They seldom talked of current friends. Some men came to the support group to find friends.

When I began presenting the workshop as a continuing education course at a local university, I frequently found more women than men attending. This prompted me to examine women's friendships. I have been listening to the stories and expectations of both men and women for many years now. It has been helpful for me to consider men and women as belonging to two slightly separate cultures, as linguist Deborah Tannen suggests.

Often, when members of a workshop break into small groups to share their ratings, the sound of their voices builds to an excited buzz. Each person explains his or her definition and why one expectation is more important than another. When they get back together in the large circle, they share the discovery that the words not only have different meanings but also have different importance depending on the kind of friendship.

June, a travel agent in her 40s, reported for her group: "We discussed what some of the words meant and never really compared, because they meant different things to different people."

Another woman reported, "We found we had different expectations, even of our sex partners."

This comment brought on a heated outpouring of discussion on whether the friendships were different depending on the sex of the individuals.

One need only to look at the results of a sample workshop (Table 1.2 as follows) to see the differences.

The men and women in this typical workshop agree on the importance of intimacy and acceptance for any friendship.

Although the men in this workshop rated commitment lower than in most, I find significant differences between men and women in every workshop. Men want to feel relaxed with their male friends and with their own partners; they want to feel complicit with their other-sex friends and their partners. However, commitment is not as important to them as it is to women.

This exercise leads to two discoveries. Each of us has unspoken but definite expectations of friendship. It is important to recognize that expectations may be different for the other person in the pair. It would be helpful to use these same words to discover some common qualities of friendship.

Table 1.2. Ratings Of Friendship Expectations By Friendship Workshop

| | Friends of Same-Sex | | Friends of Other-Sex | | Significatnt Partner | |
	Men	Women	Men	Women	Men	Women
Commitment	2	5	2	7*	2	7
Intimacy	6	7	7	7*	7	6
Relaxation	7	4	4	3	5	3
Courage	4	4	3	4	3	4
Engagement	1	2	1	2	1	2
Complicity	3	2	5	2	5	1
Acceptance	5	7	7	7*	6	5

*Where the average rating is the same, duplicates are listed and the next rating is skipped.

The Qualities Of Friendship

Picture friendship as a *creative act* by two people binding their expectations together to form a new chemical compound. Recall that Alistair Cooke called it "emotional chemistry." We say of an encounter, "The chemistry was great," or "There just wasn't any chemistry." The new compound is *friendship* composed of the emotional contributions of the two.

To interpret the process of friendship, we need to understand the interplay of emotions, thought processes and physical responses. Our million-year-old genetic chemistry — including the heart-pounding euphoria, the blush and more — makes us experience pleasurable feelings in "belonging" to another person, a family, a small band or a tribe.

But we are getting ahead of ourselves. First we need to be clear about what we want. Let's take a longer look at the seven words.

Commitment

Early in a relationship an intentional or unconscious commitment is made. A priority is set on the amount of time and emotional energy that will be devoted to the relationship. The commitment in an acquaintanceship is different from commitment in a friendship. Acquaintances are more catch-as-catch-can while friendships are more intentional.

Recall how loosely we use the word "friend." Friendship is a relationship, but it is also an emotion like loneliness. Often it is accompanied by a feeling of sacrifice.

Setting priorities produces a hierarchy. Time and effort are not limitless: lovers, children and parents may feel slighted by others in their circle of developing friendships. Something has to give to make room for the growing friendship.

I often hear men complain that they sacrificed their friendships when they married. For these men, a new priority arrangement developed dependent on the wife's friendships. To maintain their prior friendships, these men faced the alternative of sacrificing a portion of the time spent with their wives.

A woman described how one of her friends constantly broke appointments. "We all know she is that way," she explained, "but she has other qualitites we like so we put up with her lack of dependability." I didn't ask, but I wondered how deep their commitment was to one another.

Men may rate commitment as a low expectation because they are afraid of it. However, research on couples by Susan Boland of Lock Haven University indicated that how much a man is committed to a relationship is a determining factor in whether it breaks up. The woman's commitment level had no effect. Commitment to a woman may remind men of their attempt to separate from attachment to mother.

Frequently, a friendship will unravel when one partner perceives that he or she is making many more sacrifices than the other. From a cost/benefit standpoint, commitment can be measured by what each person is putting into the friendship as well as what they are getting out of it.

The !Kung San of the Kalahari Desert practice a form of prioritizing their friendships through arrow giving. If a !Kung San hunter uses a "loaned" arrow to kill an animal, the animal belongs to the arrow owner. He or she has the honor of distributing the meat among the camp according to priority of friendship. The hunter thus shows his friendship with the arrow owner. (All hunters are male, but arrow givers are both sexes.)

Professors Phillips and Goodall observe that artists and musicians can find time for their own privacy *and* for intense one-on-one contact easier than mainstream professionals and managers: "People simply do not want to get too close to people who might make them uncomfortable by making demands on their time and emotions." So we keep our distance, afraid of the sacrifice we may be expected to make.

Intimacy

Intimacy is another abused or overused word. Yet it has been my experience that you cannot have intimacy without feeling you are *risking being rejected*.

On a night flight from Atlanta to Albuquerque, I sat next to a young woman in her 20s who was going to visit her parents. It didn't take long for her to become quite frank about her cross-sex relationships, her sex life and her problems at work. By the time we landed I knew more about her life and her family than her own family. Our eyes met once while she picked up her baggage. She looked away quickly. The "intimacy at 30,000 feet" was over.

Similar "intimacy" can be experienced at a weekend workshop where the attendees have a slim expectancy of ever meeting each other again. High altitude or weekend workshop intimacy may be cathartic but it isn't real intimacy. Intimacy often involves a fear that a significant person in your life may disapprove. Recall how you may have had someone, a parent or sibling, to whom you could "spill your guts." What caused that to end? Did you get some — perhaps very subtle — message of disapproval?

Everyone needs someone to whom he or she can spill out innermost feelings, frustrations, embarrassments. Often this is not the most significant person in one's life. Expressions of intimacy appear different for men and women.

Men's Intimacy

Even the most shallow female acquaintance can be the recipient of a man's most intimate secrets, but why do men seem to fear sharing such intimacies with other men? American men are used to expressing such emotions to their mothers. Almost any woman can serve in this capacity if she is not perceived as a threat.

Another man, on the other hand, is more likely to be a threat because his betrayal can destroy job or social opportunities. My freshman roommate in high school told my secrets around the school. I learned about betrayal and keeping my feelings to myself. Most boys learn their emotional reserve in high school, while most girls learn that intimacy creates connection.

Sociologist Michael McGill concluded that intimacy is the only criterion of close attachment. "There is no intimacy in most male friendships and none of what intimacy offers: solace and support," he states. "[Furthermore] the friendship of two women is true friendship." According to McGill, when men are accused of lacking intimacy, their response is that women "do not recognize or appreciate the ways in which men are loving . . . women set the rules for what they will or will not accept as intimate behavior, and the rules are unfair."

Women's Intimacy

Comparing the two sexes, psychologist Phillip Shaver and colleagues found that men talked about personal subjects and shared problems with same-sex friends much less than women. Men shared activities more while women shared problems more. Interestingly, men expressed appreciation of their same-sex friends more than women did of their friends. However, women are much more likely to send little signs of appreciation such as cards or flowers.

Intimacy Between The Sexes

When it comes to cross-sex intimacy, men's minds are on physical contact: being in touch. They feel appreciation for their cross-sex partner, but do not express it. They would much rather share activity rather than talk about personal subjects. Women feel more comfortable with same-sex friends, men with other-sex friends. But Shaver concluded that intimacy for both men and women focuses on appreciation and affection rather than self-disclosure. Men have a much more difficult time expressing the appreciation and affection they really do feel.

McGill identifies sex, giving, touch, intellectualizing and listening as the ways men show intimacy with women. How do men learn these behaviors? Boys sense a lot of their emotions through their *sex* organ. Few women report experiencing the "mind of its own" relationship with their genitals that boys endure.

Giving is what men do to get love. Courting through gifts and paying for the date translates to buying love.

Touch is what men do to excite women to get love.

Intellectualizing as a sign of intelligence is a quality women seek for partnership, according to Heather Trexler Remoff. This activity also prevents vulnerability and hurt for the man.

Listening is what women say they want. Men feed back what they think women want to hear.

In one sense, then, men are trained by women in their vocabulary of love. Trained by first trying to please Mother, then extending it to other women. And confusing love and friendship in doing so.

If we use McGill's definition of male intimacy, men can only intellectualize or listen with other men, no sex, touch or giving. Intellectualizing is one-upmanship and listening is hard to do when you are used to competing. Men learn a different definition of intimacy. No wonder so many of the men in my sample sought sex or pornography when they were lonely. Sex means attachment for these men.

The Paradox Of Touching

While discussing intimacy in a men's support group, a man named Ben interrupted, "I just had one of those 'ah-ha' experiences. I wondered why I stopped touching males during high school and I realized that's when touch became very aggressive in sports. Touch was competitive with males but felt real good with females." The other men in the circle added to the paradox of sports. They concluded that sports provides camaraderie and distancing at the same time. All of the men agreed that physical intimacy was a corollary of psychological intimacy. Bill said, "If you don't feel safe enough to touch, you can't feel safe enough to share your feelings."

Thus intimacy has a sexual component in most men's minds. The protocol of male sports allows them to touch only aggressively or during spontaneous celebrations. One support group ended its meetings with a circle of men, arms around each other's shoulders. One man could not join the circle; instead he yelled at us from the outside. He could not touch other men in such a safe setting. Neither could he reveal his anxieties about homophobia.

Male friendship, in one sense, is most difficult because the attraction has no sense of sexual infatuation — the chemistry is different. On the other hand, sexuality is frequently the ghost at the banquet in male-female friendships. In one of my recent workshops, one woman chose to sit out the closing circle because she could not touch a person of either sex.

Touch is used in many ways to denote contact with another: "keep in touch," "reach out and touch," "a touching" performance. Notice how often men and women, distracted, waiting for a stoplight, for example, will pat, scratch, probe or rearrange themselves.

In growing up, women have usually experienced a social world where keeping in touch produced their community. Men experienced the same world as distancing because touch was dangerous. Still, men hunger for touch as much as women.

Intimacy has a physical component but also a more profound psychological one. As Ferdinard Mount observes:

> Intimacy always entails personal authority. In a truly intimate relationship one person makes unique claims upon another, claims for services, affection, respect and attention which can be supplied only by that other person. . . . For authority in this sense does not depend upon inequality nor does it wither away under the beneficent rays of equality. *It depends solely upon one person acknowledging another person's right to make claims on him.*

You can't have intimacy without commitment.

Relaxation

Relaxation connotes a sense of equality, an environment in which barriers are down, armor is shed and masks are off. *Feelings of equality, safety and trust are required for relaxation.* Often vulnerability is associated with relaxation: letting down the guard. Men find difficulty in feeling safe with other men — they must always be on their guard, performing.

Heat Moon, author of *Blue Highways*, describes a friendship in which he did not have to compete. His friend was moving a heavy rock and Moon did not show off his strength by helping. "Nothing showed our friendship better than that rock I walked away from."

In an interview with author David Michaelis, Eunice Kennedy Shriver described the relaxation between John Kennedy and a boyhood buddy: "[The relationship] was a complete liberation of the spirit . . . President Kennedy was a completely liberated man when he was with Lem (Le Moyne Billings)." Kennedy felt safe enough to play elaborate jokes on Billings, which included a brief refusal by the Secret Service to allow Billings to see Kennedy the night he was elected president.

One man compared a friendship with another man to "walking on eggs." The two men had found companionship but were afraid to do anything — touch or say something — which might disturb the other. They were unable to relax together.

It is possible that men rate relaxation more important than women do because they find it more difficult to attain. Women appear to take it for granted in their interactions. The body language is deceiving. In same-sex small groups, the women move closer to one another while the men are stretched out, apparently more relaxed, but with their whole bodies separating one another. Women's heads are almost touching. The women achieve an intimacy in which they ping-pong conversation around the group. The men, arms folded across their chests, struggle with conversation, often allowing one man to dominate. Their apparent spread-out, open configuration belies a relaxed attitude.

Courage

It takes courage to confront a crisis in a friendship and not take an easy way out. *Courage means risking the relationship.*

Several years ago, Dave and Ron had an experience which changed the way they viewed themselves and men's roles. At a birthday party for Dave's wife, when they found no female dance partners available, they decided to slow dance together. Ron laughed, recalling, "Our hardest time was deciding who would lead and who would follow. It gave both of us a great insight into women's dependency and men's performance roles. The man always had to be in charge. The woman could just relax and be led. So we traded off roles."

The men found they had erotic feelings for each other following the experience. "A few days later we got together to talk about our feelings and admitted we were scared about the intimacy," said David. "But that was okay. *Once we acknowledged our feelings we decided there was no need to act them out."*

The openness in their friendship showed great courage: to admit feelings, to discuss them and to decide they didn't have to act on their fantasies. How many times have friendships drifted apart because the participants were afraid that confronting a problem would strain the compatibility already established? In fearing to risk looking at our feelings, we distance ourselves.

When a developing friendship gets rocky and you sense a barrier to being in touch, what do you do? When you feel a relationship is getting out of control, do you back off — attempt an
escape? Or do you face what is bothering you and then explain to
your friend what is going on? Courage is the willingness to
communicate with yourself and your friend. Every friendship is
threatened at some time by estrangement. *Getting deeper requires the
courage to face rejection.*

As a friendship gets more intense it is often accompanied by
feelings of anxiety. Reluctance to move forward and awkwardness
frequently appear as the relationship moves through new layers
of intimacy.

Dan Ackroyd reminisced about his friend John Belushi, "John
and I used to have disagreements and arguments, but they were
diffused very, very quickly because we both could take a good
scolding from each other, which is sometimes what we needed.
He snapped me in line, I snapped him in line."

Engagement

Many workshop attendees have trouble with the concept of engagement. Several have said, "I don't care whether someone thinks
about me or not." Neither the men nor the women in the sample
workshop rated engagement very high. *Yet thinking about someone does
reflect a progressing attachment.* This develops from a history of words,
jokes and behaviors unique to that relationship. One author called
it "prizing." Phillips and Goodall observe, "You can identify a strong
friendship by its history and the nature of its talk."

We telephone our close friends frequently. These relationships
are different from our once- or twice-a-year friends, our long-
distance friends, our Christmas-card friends. Telephoning has
replaced the letter. Both are used much more frequently by for-
eign-born residents.

Several years ago I interviewed an economist from Iran who
had a nationwide support group of Iranian friends linked by daily
long-distance calls. I thought that his telephone bill was outra-
geous, but he said, "It is worth every minute which I have with
my friends." His friends were such that he could ask them to come
live with and look after his wife and children while he was away.

How often do we think of our friends? Every few hours, every day or less frequently? Commitment requires physical time and effort, but *engagement goes further, requiring a place in one's heart.* Men can think frequently of a female attachment, but can they just as easily reserve an equal spot for a male friend? Women are known for recognizing this feeling and doing something about it. But there are few instances when male friendships approach the intensity of communication of female friendships.

Complicity

There is a time in most true friendships when *the "me" becomes the "we."* During adolescence, boys develop buddyships and girls cluster in cliques. From their point of view they feel they are forming a necessary conspiracy against the world. Each member excites the other to greater feats of daring and excellence. True friends don't deny or denigrate their companion's successes, but take some pride in their accomplishments. These conspirators consider doing anything for one another.

The conspirators feel they share a commonality. Their values, mores and ideals appear the same. Complicity demands this equality. As C.S. Lewis observed:

> Friendship arises out of mere companionship when two or more of the companions discover that they have in common some insight or interest or even taste which the others do not share and which, till that moment, each believed to be his own unique treasure [or burden].

This is the feeling which frequently circles around a gathering of men when they realize that they are not alone in their loneliness. Complicity is the most active of the descriptors of friendship and the most *masculine* identified. Sherrod calls it sensual-active association because doing frequently allows touching: adolescent mischief, sports, military, work and drinking, to list a few activities. Assistance and generosity, support and nourishing are expected even if unasked for. This "doing together" is explicit in the many buddy films Hollywood says we want. *The Sting* and *Butch Cassidy and the Sundance Kid* are classic examples to which *Steel Magnolias* and *Thelma and Louise* must be added.

Acceptance

Everyone wants acceptance because it means belonging — attachment. *It is the realization that in spite of what I think are my faults and foibles, I am appreciated.*

Acceptance is the most frequent expectation voiced in my workshops and is the only criterion common to our list in Table 1.1. One woman in her 50s who came to a workshop with her husband called it "unconditional love." It is the unconditional love we expected from our parents.

Most workshop attendees say, "I want to be accepted as I am." They say their public lives feel like a performance. They may even feel like impostors. They need a safe place where their ordinary, human failures and frailties are *overlooked* by a significant attachment.

In reality we do place conditions on our friendships, which I am calling expectations. We do share values and beliefs. It is hard to get past the first stages of companionship otherwise. Nevertheless we also accept some behaviors in our friends which disturb us. *Resolving these conflicts is how we become better friends.* Acceptance is one method of resolution. But carried too far it can become co-dependency — enabling the friends to continue the "unacceptable behavior."

A friend who feels like a "twin" hardly creates the chemistry for which we search. Being complementary, the rubbing together of two different individuals produces the warmth of friendship. Differences must be accepted. In a friendship each person must accept the other, but also accept himself or herself. To expect the other to change for you or for you to change for the other's approval denies each person's individuality.

I have had a long-standing friendship with a restaurant owner of my own age. During the Persian Gulf intervention, he was on one side of the debate and I was on the other. We were very clear about our opposing positions, but this did not affect our friendship. We continue to accept and don't try to change the other.

Not trying to fix things is a sign of friendship, according to Henri Nouwen.

> The friend who can be silent with us in a moment of despair or confusion, who can stay with us in an hour of grief, who can

tolerate not knowing, not curing, not healing, and face with us the reality of our powerlessness, that is the friend who cares.

Another of David Michaelis' examples of friendship is the competitive camaraderie between two Navy officers, Leonard Picotte and Michael Edwards. To advance in the military service they had to compete for top grades at each naval station. Such tension created a pushing match, which they later called the "Battle of the Kitchen." In spite of the battle, or possibly because of it, they discovered friendship their top priority. Picotte says: "You gotta have somebody. And I mean a nonsexual friend. There's only so much that you'll tell your whoever, and at that point you need that kind of guy with whom you can just really truly be yourself. That's the purest kind of relationship. There's nothing asked, nothing expected, nothing to cloud it up. There are no pressures from the biology of the thing. I accept him as he accepts me."

Disapproval: A Test

The most difficult test of friendship is to disapprove of inappropriate behavior and yet accept the individual involved. To separate the friendship and, therefore, the friend from the activity. Here lies a paradox between commitment and acceptance. We can always find reasons for not approving of our friends if they don't live up to our expectations. Why aren't they smarter, more sensitive, more athletic, less athletic, less busy?

Where their behavior impinges on friendship, do we have the courage to say, "I need more of your attention"? Where their activity disturbs our ideals or values, but not the relationship, can we say, "I don't like what you're doing, but you are still my friend"?

Same-sex friendships are often more stable and friends more accepting than "lovers."

Acceptance is also being with a friend without having to do something — even talk. Men, being activity oriented, want a reason to be together. But just to sit, feet up on a ledge, watching the wind polish the water or the clouds scrub the sky is hard to do. It's hard for men to stop performing and relax even for a few moments.

What Have We Learned From
Trying To Put Words To The Ineffable?

When asked, we can put words and descriptions to friendship. However, these words have different meanings. Men and women have somewhat different expectations. These differences are added to the differences which rise out of our separate growing-up experiences with our parents. We are unique individuals with different expectations searching for connections.

A re-examination of men's expectations of friendship may contribute to a redefinition of masculinity. Men are going to have to do the redefining. Women's input will be helpful, but men must examine their needs from their own biosocial perspectives and not try to please women. The same must be said for women. They must take care of their needs first and not try to please men.

If we want to experience the challenge of cross-sex friendships, the first step in resolving our gender differences is to recognize and accept them and not expect either sex to conform to the other's expectations. Linguist Deborah Tannen finds it helpful to regard men and women as two separate cultures. We are not going to change these cultures, at least not in our lifetimes, so we must learn to communicate our expectations to one another. Our most frequent error is to assume that the other *knows* what we want.

Now that we have explored a wide spectrum of thought about friendship, ask yourself:

- Would you like to reconsider your expectations of friendship?
- Something great just happened to you, who are you going to tell?
- Who will you call when your doctor tells you to come back for more tests after your annual checkup?
- What friends do you want to visit you while recovering in the hospital?
- When you wake up frightened at 3:00 AM, whom can you call?
- How would you respond to a friend who called you at 3:00 AM?
- What do you contribute to your friendships?
- What are your strengths and weaknesses?
- Really, what is important to you in a friendship?

CHAPTER · TWO

Admitting
We Are Lonely

— * —

Give me a hunger
O you gods who sit and give
The world its orders,
Give me hunger, pain and want . . .

But leave me a little love,
A voice to speak to me in the day end,
A hand to touch me in the dark room
Breaking the long loneliness.

— Carl Sandburg

The Journey Toward Friendship Begins

Loneliness is the emotion which drives our personal lives and colors our national image. It is so much a part of our lives and culture that we often ignore or discount it, not wishing to embrace the possibility that we are not very good at making warm attachments. We feel, at some level, that we have failed, and are embarrassed at our ineptitude at making those important connections others seem to make so easily. To admit our failure seems to compound the pain of loneliness.

The pain of those missing attachments can be used constructively, however, to turn loneliness into a positive force that draws us toward necessary and healthy links with others. If we are able to admit that we are lonely and to experience the pain of missing attachments, we can begin to get over it.

In loneliness, as in other unhappy states, the first step in healing the pain is to explore its source.

Coping With Loneliness

After presenting *Making Friendships* workshops for several years for both men and women, I discovered by accident the link between loneliness and the behaviors we use to cope with the pain. It was one of those "Eureka!" experiences which are so obvious afterward that change your life.

"Addiction is a way of avoiding painful feelings, a way of numbing out," said Louis, the therapist leading my men's support group. *"What are your addictions?"*

Jack, an unmarried college professor, blurted out, "I'm trying to fix my loneliness with TV. I know I could abuse alcohol when I'm alone — my father was an alcoholic. So I use the TV to numb my loneliness." Men's heads began bobbing up and down like those glass novelty birds drinking water.

Bob, a 35-year-old software expert, interrupted, "I used TV, too, when my wife and two-year-old went to visit her parents. I came to the meeting tonight because I was lonely. I find other things to do than the tube now."

Roger, an epidemiologist, added, "I'm addicted to relationships. But that doesn't work. I look for women, any woman, to take care of my loneliness." More heads bobbing.

Bob became excited. "Yeah, I did that too. I went to women for wrapping . . . you know, hugging and touching. I needed the touching. I thought it was the sex."

Albert, new to the group, spoke for the first time. "I just came here to listen. I have a hard time sharing my feelings but you're all so open." He paused as if building up courage. "I'm going through a divorce after 26 years of marriage. I travel a lot and I used women and alcohol for my loneliness." He paused again and lowered his voice. "It didn't work."

Pete, a programmer, had kept silent. Now when we looked at him for a comment, he spoke. "I guess you can tell I use food." The other men laughed politely. Pete was about a hundred pounds overweight. "I can't keep any food in the house. And I read a lot . . . as many books as I can afford. So I stuff myself when I am lonely . . . with food or facts, you know?"

The revelation traveled around the room, each man admitting some behavior which he thought treated his loneliness. One was seeing a lawyer the next day to end a marriage. The modulated voices suggested that these men were either resigned to the pain of loneliness or they were sharing something very secret — the shame of loneliness and how they masked it, even from themselves.

I sensed a feeling of rejection — self-rejection and rejection by others. I resolved to find out more about loneliness, my loneliness as well as others.

How pervasive is this feeling of loneliness?

Who is lonely and why?

Is there a connection between loneliness and addiction?

Or was this just a self-selected group of men outside of what society considers "normal"?

I began by questioning those who attended my *Making Friendships* workshops.

A First Workshop

The room begins to fill.

They arrive at their first workshop quietly and singly, and take seats separate from one another. Some come directly from work, still conservatively dressed. Others are more casually attired in jeans.

After introducing myself and the workshop, I ask them to answer two questions anonymously on a three-by-five card:

- Why did you come to this workshop?
- What do you expect to get out of it?

When the cards are handed in, I shuffle and redistribute them to others. Then I say, "Please tell us your name, where you live and read the card as if it is your answer to the questions."

After they have gone around the circle I ask, "What did you learn from doing the exercise?"

Carol, a honey blond in her thirties, responds quickly: "We are all here for about the same reason. We don't have close friends or partners . . . and we want to learn how to find them."

Sandra, slightly overweight, in her early twenties, confesses, "Some of us admitted we were lonely and didn't have any friends. I thought I was the only one."

Loneliness

Many of us feel like the only lonely person in the world — and believe it's so. The pervasive feeling of isolated singularity can be a major influence on our lives. The people in the support group were not unique in their loneliness; they were only unique in their willingness to express it openly.

You can join in the process of the group by completing the questionnaire in Appendix A (page 247).

The Extent Of Loneliness

- More than forty percent of single men and women consider loneliness the greatest disadvantage of being single.
- About one-fifth of U.S. teenagers feel "very lonely, empty, so lonely I would rather die."
- Americans in the 25 to 44 age group are showing more acute depressive episodes than any other age group. One would expect that the older the person, the more opportunities for depression. This is not the case.
- It is a myth that the elderly are more lonely. Many elderly people have developed coping skills to deal with the problems of loneliness. Those over 45 who attend my workshops are less likely to admit to being frequently lonely than are younger people.
- We blame ourselves — our social skills — for being lonely.

When we learn to identify the expectations we place on our relationships, we can begin to change our social behaviors. These changes, in turn, may well affect the way others respond to us. The old maxim holds true: "I cannot change others. All I can change is myself."

By changing my own social behaviors, I can be the catalyst of change in the responses of others.

Loneliness Is A Positive Emotion

The first discovery about loneliness is very important, yet quite simple: It's OK to feel lonely. After more than 20 years of observation and study, I have come to the conclusion that loneliness can be a positive emotion which tells us we need human attachment. We may arrive at this realization kicking and screaming with pain or wincing with denial. No matter how we come to accept the fact of loneliness, it is the acceptance that makes the difference.

Depression And Loneliness

Sometimes loneliness is really depression, so it is important to distinguish between "normal" loneliness — the lack of human attachments — and the emotional suffering associated with clinical depression. The words we use to describe loneliness are often the same as those that describe symptoms of clinical depression: emptiness, sadness, pain, alienation, desperation, hopelessness, failure, powerlessness and worthlessness. However, clinical depression is often accompanied by other debilitating symptoms, which may include any number of the following:

1. Loss of interest or pleasure in ordinary activities, including sex
2. Sleep disturbances (insomnia, early-morning waking, over-sleeping)
3. Eating disturbances (changes in appetite and/or weight loss or gain)
4. Decreased energy, fatigue
5. Restlessness, irritability
6. Difficulty in concentrating, remembering, making decisions
7. Thoughts of death or suicide.

If you experience four or more of the above symptoms — including some of the loneliness-associated words — for more than two weeks, you might question whether you are more than just lonely. Perhaps it is an indication that you should consider seeking professional help.

A Working Definition

Loneliness is a feeling. It is a response to our relationship with others.

Being alone is an experience, not necessarily connected to emotional coloration. Being alone can be pleasant, unpleasant or neutral. It reflects our relationship with ourselves.

Loneliness is the state of feeling alone when we don't want to be alone. This definition implies that we feel emotionally dissatisfied, disconnected from others, lacking in human attachment — whether we are, in fact, alone or in the company of others. We can be with people and still feel lonely. The experience of feeling alone at those times does not fulfill our emotional expectations and needs.

Every person I have questioned can easily differentiate between "loneliness" and "being alone." A large majority add that being alone at times is absolutely necessary — and extremely enjoyable. The experience of being alone can be attended with a wonderful sense of well-being, of being at peace with yourself, of feeling centered and unified. This is quite different from feeling lonely.

Writing about loneliness is not new. In the seventeenth century Robert Burton concluded in *The Anatomy of Melancholy* that melancholy was an "inbred malady in every one of us." Its cause was "Enforced solitariness [of those who] must abandon all company . . . and cannot have company, as many of our country gentlemen do in solitary houses, they must either be alone without companions [or] spend their time with lewd fellows in taverns and in alehouses, and thence addict themselves to some unlawful disports or dissolute courses."

Today there are many choices between these extremes, many ways to reach out for friendship to alleviate our loneliness. But making friends is a learning process which may require a great deal of effort.

Our society's ideal is loving families, supportive communities and ethnic groups merging with each other. Yet we find ways of isolating ourselves. Novelist D.H. Lawrence described the American experience as reflected in our literature: "The essential American soul is hard, isolate, stoic and a killer."

We live paradoxical lives — needing to belong and yet to be separate. Coping with this paradox of attachment and autonomy is central to the task of learning to be friends.

Loneliness arises from lack of attachment and is usually identified as a negative emotion. Solitude, on the other hand, is an opportunity to be separate, to be alone with one's self, to enjoy the sense of the whole, to be autonomous. Solitude is chosen, loneliness seems unavoidable.

Where Does It Start?

The newborn, violently detached from the womb, confronts an alien environment where solace and basic needs are provided by the primary care person, usually the mother. As the child's world expands, its connections with a father figure and others become important for its developing skills of attachment and separation.

Ideally, the preadult years should be a balance of secure attachment and separate exploration. During these years we learn and practice our friendship skills.

How well we have learned and now practice these skills is reflected in our answers to the questionnaire (Appendix A). These answers will show us how we cope with loneliness just as they have for those attending the workshops.

1. How Frequently Do You Feel Lonely?

Participants were asked to record how often they felt lonely — a few times a year, once or twice a month, once or twice a week, nearly every day, daily?

I classified people who admitted feeling lonely once or twice a week or more as lonely. The data showed this represented 44 percent of the men and 30 percent of the women. I also asked these people to rate relationships with their peers.

Sandra, the woman who thought she was the only one in the room who was lonely, was wrong. About half of the people who attend workshops are likely to feel lonely.

Before I began asking these questions, I believed that men were less likely than women to admit being lonely. It was surprising to find the opposite was true. Sixty-one percent of the men attending friendship workshops assessed themselves as feeling lonely once or twice a week or more, while less than half of the women did.

However, male and female workshop attendees did not differ significantly in their assessment of their peer relationships, even though more men said that their peer relationships were below average.

The difference between men and women in self-reported loneliness is striking. While women generally have a better support system than men, they are attracted to my workshops, they say, to understand better what men want in a friendship. Men are

more likely to attend in order to seek a woman in a nonthreaten-
ing environment.

Table 2.1. Who Is Lonely?

| | Percent | | | |
| | Those who are lonely once or twice a week or more | | Those who rate their peer relations below average | |
	Men	Women	Men	Women
Students	29	17	21	6
Friendship workshop	61	45	43	32
Others (therapists, yoga class, friends)	17	24	24	7
In a partnership	26	20	22	11
Single or divorced	49	32	36	15

Women are surprised to find that men want the same things
they do, such as attention and affection. However, men find themselves trapped in the roles they think they must play. As we shall
see, these roles are somewhat different from those the women
want them to play.

2. When Are You Lonely?

There are times during the week when you are more likely to
feel lonely. At some of these times you can do something about it,
like calling a friend. At other times you may have to find alterna-
tives. People answering this question were directed to "check as
many as apply." In doing so, many of them checked five or more
of the conditions.

There was little difference between men and women in the
conditions, with two exceptions: women were significantly more
lonely late at night, men were more lonely at work (see Table 2.2).

Table 2.2. When Are You Lonely?

	Percent	
	Men	**Women**
At work	37	25
After work	49	45
In the evening	62	59
Late at night	50	62
On the weekend	67	67
In a group of people	57	49
With a spouse or significant partner	31	33

3. How Do You Cope With Loneliness?

What do people do when lonely? The survey question asked, "Have you ever done the following while you felt lonely? Rank as many as apply by: 1 = most frequently, 2 = next frequently, 3 and so on." The choices are listed as follows, in Table 2.3.

Women choose to work or shop significantly more frequently than men when they are lonely. Men seek sex or pornography much more frequently than women when they are lonely. Men and women are similar in their other choices. There are some behaviors in this list which, if they were abused, could become addictions or excessive attachments. Eating, drinking alcohol, using drugs, seeking sex or pornography and even working can be damaging to your health or your relationships with your loved ones. I classify them "risky behaviors."

Workshop attendees often express relief when they learn of these results. Sally, a 35-year-old woman who admitted to being in therapy, said, "It's great to see I'm not alone. That others do the same crazy things I do. I thought I was the only one."

Sandra added quickly, "It's like we're all alike."

Table 2.3. How Do You Cope With Loneliness?

	Percent	
	Men	Women
Sought the company of others?	84	86
Watched more TV than usual?	80	78
Exercised?	65	68
Read a lot?	65	68
Went shopping?	40	66
Ate a lot?	58	64
Sought sex or pornography?	47	14
Worked longer than usual?	44	60
Drank a lot of alcohol?	36	31
Used drugs?	15	8

Loneliness And Health

It is easier for many of us to self-medicate the pain of loneliness with risky behavior than to chance abandonment by a potential friend or partner. We may even become chemically attached to these behaviors. If we are not chemically dependent, we can still be addicted to the chemical high associated with every one of these behaviors.

Few authors have connected loneliness with addictive behaviors and little, if any, research is available to support the anecdotal reports.

Louise Bernikow says,

> Loneliness can, indeed, make you sick. Heart disease and hyper-
> tension are now generally thought of as loneliness diseases exacer-
> bated by a person's sense of abandonment by the world, separation
> from the rest of humanity. Most addictions are also considered
> loneliness diseases, which the medical profession is beginning to
> recognize but which recovering alcoholics, drug addicts, even smok-
> ers have long been aware of. *Most addicts admit that their best friends
> have been booze, drugs or tobacco.*

The lack of an emotional support system is blatantly unhealthy.
Recent surveys of several urban and rural populations have dem-
onstrated emphatically that more socially isolated people have
two to four times the mortality rate of those with high levels of
social integration. The more socially isolated have higher rates of
tuberculosis, accidents and psychiatric disorders. Perhaps we
should be just as concerned about the poisons of loneliness as we
are about the poisons in our environment.

A recent headline read: "Living alone can prove to be hazardous
to your health." The results of two separate studies focus on the
22.6 million Americans (12 percent) who live alone. One study
found that "heart attack patients living alone were nearly twice as
likely as others to suffer another heart attack — and more likely
to die of an attack — within six months."

The other study proved that the five-year survival rate was
significantly less for "unmarried heart patients without a close
personal confidant." Others have uncovered a curious sex difference. Men who live alone are "more demoralized than those living
with others: quite different than women who are more likely to
be demoralized living with others."

What is not clear at present is whether the higher mortality
rate among the lonely is due directly to some biological difference
or whether it is the result of behaviors, including addictions,
which make the person more susceptible to disease. Divorced
men have eight times the death rate of cirrhosis of the liver and
four times as many are killed in auto accidents as married men.
There is no way to verify in all cases whether those accidents
were also influenced by alcohol.

The Dimensions Of Loneliness

Look at the words everyone associated with loneliness earlier: emptiness, sadness, pain, alienation, desperation, hopelessness, failure, powerlessness and worthlessness. Everyone seems to know how loneliness feels, but it is much harder to measure it. Are there different kinds of loneliness at different times?

Some observers of loneliness believe there are two kinds — emotional and social. I find it helpful to recognize that loneliness comes from four directions — interpersonal, social, cultural and cosmic — as first suggested by sociologist William Sadler and psychologist Thomas Johnson, Jr.

Lack of *intimates* makes up the first dimension of loneliness: that is, real friends, family and "touching attachments." In the hierarchy of human relationships we feel most comfortable touching these intimates. Here is where our understanding of attachment begins. We all know what it feels like not to have someone who cares about us.

The "Out Group"

Our *social environment* also gives us a sense of belonging, whether it is in clubs, associations, neighborhoods, classrooms or the workplace. It is where one considers interpersonal contacts to be "friends" when they are more likely to be colleagues, acquaintances or buddies.

The "out group" — the estranged — are all more susceptible to this dimension of loneliness. Women, African-Americans, foreigners and the handicapped, among others, have experienced this type of loneliness.

Clubs, secret societies with rites, passwords, handshakes and gangs are all formed to sustain a sense of belonging. While the all-male group of the past is in decline, men still gather for communal identity as sports fans, in the neighborhood tavern, for noon lunches and in their exclusively male sports teams. On the street, the gang is just a modification of normal behavior. It creates its own tribe with self-decoration, new names and language, hazing, exploiting younger boys, sex and fertility symbols, death and rebirth rites. Rare is the human who has outgrown the need to belong to a tribe.

Belonging And Xenophobia

The *cultural dimension* considers people's relationship with their traditions. Nationalism, statism, regionalism and tribalism all give the individual a feeling of belonging — a sense of origin. The healthy end of the spectrum might be to wear costumes from one's country of origin, while xenophobia might appear at the unhealthy end of the spectrum.

In this age of the "global village," a financial hiccup in Japan's economic indicators can affect stock markets and VCR sales in the U.S. and Germany. A drought in Russia can mean a year of healthy sales for U.S. farmers. Humans are just a few thousand years separated from their million-year hunting and gathering heritage. Besides being linked to our little tribes, humans are becoming sensitized to consider themselves as citizens of the world. What people do in one country can pollute the air or water in another, causing destruction of the oceans and the rain forests. The leap in global identity is too much for most of us.

The list of those who cannot seem to get along with their neighbors is endless: Protestants and Catholics in Northern Ireland, Catholics and Moslems in Lebanon, Jews and Arabs in the Middle East. In India, Moslems, Hindus and Sikhs feud endlessly. With dissolution of the great Russian hegemony of Eastern Europe, former nations are fragmenting into smaller and smaller ethnic enclaves. In the United States, Southerners have yet to lay the Civil War to rest, still battling over the continued presence of the Confederate flag. Northern Californians routinely threaten secession. Only when catastrophe occurs do we suspend our provincialism and sense our attachment to all humanity.

There is abundant evidence of cultural attachment. We stridently resist denying our cultural attachments and wholeheartedly approve of those who wrap themselves in the national flag. The war in the Persian Gulf brought most Americans together for a moment in time. Violence, whether on the battlefield or the playing field, is an attachment ritual.

In the football stadiums around the country, from the smallest high school to the Super Bowl, we scream for the opposing players to be killed or maimed. We are fascinated by the violence, raising our voices in a deafening roar and our bodies in great waves. At these emotional moments we belong.

This "violence of belonging," depicted so well in movies about war and sports, spreads from the playing fields into the stands, penetrating into the fans themselves. At soccer games in Europe and post-game brawls in the United States, the common adrenaline surge of violence brings us together.

A Higher Power

All religions attempt to gather things together to create a sense of meaning and belonging. Religion attempts to answer the question, "Why am I here?" In the same way, we all attempt to create a personal mythology. Canadian loneliness investigator Daniel Perman said, "Existential loneliness may be more tied to the lack of religion or meaning in life than to a lack of interpersonal bonds."

The Speaker in Ecclesiastes, after seeking wisdom, wealth and pleasure, concludes, "I saw that everything was emptiness and chasing the wind, of no profit under the sun." After rambling through his attempts to find meaning to his life, he laments, "In my empty existence I have seen it all." His advice to the young is "Remember your Creator in the days of your youth, before the time of trouble comes and the years draw near when you will say, 'I see no purpose in them.'"

The cosmically lonely experience a purposeless life: a life of the "theater of the absurd," as represented by the dark drama of Camus, Albee, Beckett, Pinter and Shepard.

Anomia

Sadler and Johnson suggest that if we feel deprivation in two or more of these dimensions, we suffer a more profound loneliness called *anomia*. This feeling of "normlessness" is also described as meaninglessness, emptiness, valuelessness or powerlessness.

Consideration of *anomia* may help to explain the pervasive feeling of loneliness in America today.

My own experience of *anomia* developed years ago, when I took my family to La Jolla, California, to do research at the Salk Institute, a center of scientific ferment. Two months before we left Atlanta for California, Dr. Martin Luther King, Jr., was killed. One of the greatest funerals I ever witnessed wound through the streets of my hometown.

On the night we arrived in La Jolla, Bobby Kennedy was killed. During that year, the Santa Barbara oil spill occurred and I found oil-covered dead birds washed ashore in La Jolla, 200 miles to the south. The People's Park riot in Berkeley, the police riot at the Chicago Democratic Convention, the Tet offensive in Vietnam, the Paris riots, the Prague spring and the Russian summer also twisted my perspectives. Drugs were used openly along California beaches and at middle-class parties.

When I returned to Atlanta in 1969, there was a mini-Haight/ Ashbury on Peachtree Street and a police riot in Piedmont Park. My culture was breaking down.

Culture Shock

While in California I realized that I did not have the political or social abilities to complement my scientific curiosity and felt like an outsider in the company of my scientific peers. Fortunately, during that year I found a spiritual home in the Religious Society of Friends and my family became much closer. But when we returned to Atlanta, the children spun off to their own teenage culture and my wife to jobs treating teenage drug users. Like most men, I had no intimate friends. To compound my loneliness, my mentor died of cancer. I couldn't diagnose it at the time, but I was suffering from a classic case of *anomia*. My culture was alien, my social environment was unsupportive and I had no intimates.

Other scientists report experiencing such culture shock, especially when studying primitive peoples in remote places. My friend Jean is a prime example. After she spent six months in 1976 in Botswana with the !Kung San, a primitive society, she felt embarrassed and anxious returning to her own affluent home and

wealthy community. She needed a workshop of other people involved in alternative lifestyles to help her reintegrate.

Culture shock was frequently seen in returning Peace Corps
volunteers by therapist Donald Ottenberg. It can also be treated
through support groups. He observes, "There is a clash of values
of the small tribal community that the volunteer has been part of
with the ego-centered, self-seeking, competitive and aggressive
norms of many people in the United States."

Homeless And *Anomia*

The same symptoms appear in homeless "street people" and in
big league baseball players. Homelessness is much like being
"shipwrecked; [it] is unaffiliation or disaffiliation, rejection, alienation, leftover and having no place to fit in." I admitted men and
women coming to a healthcare clinic for the homeless. While
many demanded treatment for minor ills, they were actually seeking a little bit of attention.

For celebrity athletes who are constantly traveling, there are
ever-present fears of failure and of not being accepted, making
them feel lonely and vulnerable to drugs and sex.

The Magic Johnson revelation has brought other athletes to
recognize their risky behaviors when lonely. Gwen Torrence, a
track and field medalist in the 1992 Olympics in Europe, says, "If
you see [people] together, it doesn't mean they're sleeping together.
But as time went on, I realized it's very tempting. You get very
lonely over there . . ." She observed that many female athletes
were looking for "*the* guy" even if he was married.

The Vietnam Vet

Vietnam veterans may represent the worst cases of *anomia* in
our culture. They returned to find the culture changed and hos-
tile, the social support system unrecognizable and personal relationships alien. No wonder many vets retained the drug behaviors
they used in Vietnam to cope. It is surprising that so many did
quit. In contrast, the Gulf War "heroes" were treated to great
flag-waving, parades and rhetoric.

When a person suffers loneliness in just one of the dimensions, he or she probably can compensate by using other attachments. But when one's underpinnings slide out from more than one direction, balance is harder to find and *anomia* has a good chance of setting in.

Thus far we have examined some of the parameters of loneliness. Understanding these will help in finding what our needs are. We have made the initial connection between loneliness and attachment. We have seen where missing human attachment can make us sick or make us do things which can harm us or harm our human relationships. Most important, we have learned that many of us are lonely in several dimensions and that it is okay to be lonely.

Ask yourself . . .

- What does your loneliness feel like? (What words did you rate high?)
- Have you been ignoring your loneliness? In what way? Keeping busy, etc.?
- When are you most likely to be lonely? What do you do then?
- How have you been coping with your loneliness? Can you define different dimensions of loneliness within yourself?
- Do you know anyone who appears to be lonely? What does he or she do that gives you that impression?
- What are your excuses for not treating your loneliness with friendships?

CHAPTER · THREE

When Our Models Are Missing Or Damaged

❋

My own image of a life is that of a traveler whose knapsack is slowly filled with doubts, dogma and desires during the first dozen years. Each traveler spends the adult years trying to empty the heavy load in the knapsack until he or she can confront the opportunities that are present in each fresh day. Some adults approach this state. Most carry their collection of uncertainties, prejudices, and frustrated wishes into middle and old age trying to prove what must remain uncertain while raging wildly at ghosts.

— Jerome Kagan, *The Nature of the Child*

Our parents, for better or worse, remain primary and lasting models for our relationships with others. As one author observed, "So my youthful yearning for parental approval has never slaked. Family ghosts still haunt my cortex."

My ghosts continue to haunt me in my own mid-century. My mother has been dead for nearly 30 years, my father for 20. Daily I recognize their phrases, attitudes and postures in my own life and the lives of their adult grandchildren. The experience is common.

Frank, a chiropractor in his 30s, almost wept as he confided to me, "Damn, I see my father every time I look in the mirror. Every day I find myself more like him. And I have tried so hard to not be like the SOB."

How Good Are Our Parents?

We learn friendship models from our parents and peers from birth onward. People who come to the friendship workshops are more likely to judge their preadult years with their parents and peers as unsatisfactory, at least when compared to college students. Let us examine Figure 3.1 on the following pages.

Mothers

Look at the relationships with mothers first. More college women rate their mother-daughter relationship below average during adolescence. When they are surveyed as adults, the number of disappointed women decreases from 30 percent as adolescents to 6 percent as adults.

Figure 3.1. Relationships Of Students And Worksh

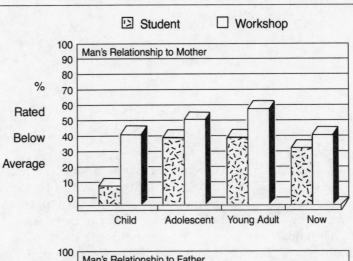

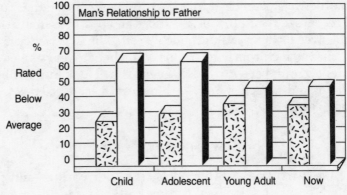

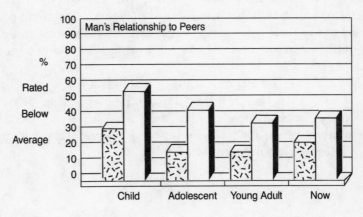

tendees To Parents And Peers During 4 Life Periods

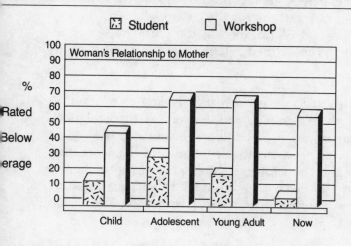

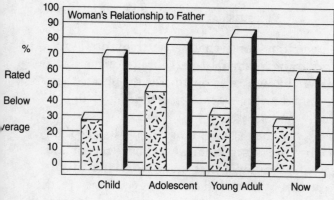

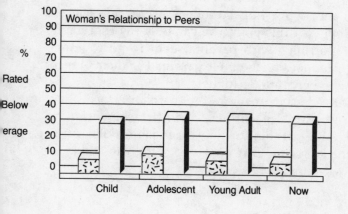

About a third of the college men report their relationships with their mothers as below average. It drops slightly for these men as adults, but not as significantly as for the college women.

In contrast, 40 percent of the men in the workshops and 55 percent of the women report their relationships with their mothers never improve.

Fathers

Relationships with dads are even worse. Nearly a constant 30 to 40 percent of both college men and women say their relationships with their fathers were, and still are, below average.

The only difference between the students and the workshop attendees is the higher percentages. Most striking is the nearly 80 percent of workshop women who judged their relationships with fathers below average when they were adolescents and young adults.

Friends

Relationships with peers fare somewhat better than those with parents. There appears to be a constant percentage of men and women who have below average relationships throughout their lives. The percentage is higher for workshop attendees than college students.

Other researchers report that students are more lonely than older respondents. Maybe students' memories are more recent and more accurate. We saw in Chapter 2 that more workshop attendees than students were lonely. The students surveyed here are at least two to three years older than the sophomores usually studied.

On the other hand, workshop attendees are a self-selected group of lonely people. At this point, we can only say that loneliness and poor relationships with parents seem to go together. Maybe workshop attendees blame their parents for their present state and so skew the percentages higher.

How we experienced attachment and its corollary, separation, during our preadult years will influence our attachments now. However, even blaming parents for poor friendship skills can be self-defeating in the long run. Our goal is to recognize and overcome this barrier with improved skills.

First, let us look at what we learn about attachment while growing up.

Paradoxical Living: Attachment And Separation

Once the umbilical cord is cut, which is the first separation, the infant still feels itself attached, that is, merged to the mother. Any separation is sensed as loss of self, and the infant protests until it is satisfied or worn out. Satisfaction is achieved through holding, cradling, touching, listening and oral gratification.

Even at this early point in development, the girl-child and boy-child are usually treated differently. The girl-child represents the same sex and, thus, the same emotional bonds as the mother has experienced in her own childhood. The boy represents the "other" and the emotional experience the mother has encountered with her father as well as the boy's father.

Sociologist/psychologist Nancy Chodorow suggests in *The Reproduction of Mothering* that "Girls, then, seem to become and experience themselves as the self of the mother's fantasy, whereas boys become the other."

Forming The Bond

Newborn infants can distinguish Mother's voice and smell from that of other mothers. This is not surprising if one considers the amount of learning taking place before birth. The fetus hears the mother's voice pattern and tastes her chemicals in the amniotic fluid.

Chemicals reach the fetus from the outside through the mother. The womb is thought to be just as permeable to sound. Infants of mothers who watched a specific TV show when pregnant were seen to recognize the theme music by responding with a "quiet alert" state.

Mother And Child

The crying infant causes a significant increase in blood pressure and skin conductance in parents (both mothers and fathers). In a paired study with nonabusive mothers, abusive mothers were significantly more annoyed by and less sympathetic toward a crying infant. They also showed increases in heart rate and skin conductance and increased anger when viewing crying as well as smiling infants.

Mothers can pick their infants out of a group simply by touch. A recent study in Jerusalem reported that about 70 percent of blindfolded mothers could recognize their newborns 5 to 72 hours after birth if they had held them for a cumulative period of one hour or more beforehand. If the baby's hands were covered, the identification didn't work.

The infant-mother interaction builds the psychobiologic pathways the individual will use throughout life, according to Tiffany Field, a child psychologist. Even before birth, the psychological and neurological connections are forming. After birth, the mother acts as stimulant and arousal modulator for the infant.

When the infant feels overstimulated, it breaks eye contact. If the mother does not recognize this, she can annoy the infant to frustration. Later, the father and then peers will act as stimulants, and the child will return to the mother for arousal modulation.

Father And Child

Lacking as it does the physical interconnectedness of the mother-infant relationship, the father-infant bond takes a different sort of effort to develop.

If emotional or other barriers prove too great for equal parenting, the father may regress to his Oedipal feelings with *his* father. Chodorow observes that, "Having a child recreates the desired mother-child exclusivity for a woman and interrupts it for a man, just as the man's father intruded into his relation to his mother."

The mother can assuage her loneliness with her infant, but the father may feel more lonely. The father should be prepared to intrude into the mother-infant pair at birth. Yet in our society, the opposite is often true: The father is assigned an away-from-the-family provider role.

Yet the father's role is of equal importance to the mother's. Through the father's attitudes, the infant learns that males can nurture also. At the same time, the father can assist in the infant's first stages of separation from the mother. He helps in the separation of self from not-self and in the child's realization of its gender identity.

Separation Anxiety

Attachment objects are constructed from the ghosts of our childhoods. The separation experience impacts our attachment needs. John Bowlby, who observed that unloved children can waste away and die, says that separation anxiety "is what each of us experiences whenever our attachment behavior is elicited and we cannot find our mother figure, or whatever person or even institution has come in later years to stand in her place."

The mind creates the images and our bodies produce the chemicals which influence the feelings of attachment and separation.

Young children at play with their caregivers nearby provide an illustration of the classic struggle between attachment and separation. After a period of vigorous exercise, the children seek out their caregivers, usually their mothers, for some attention. They may climb into a lap, but after a short period, which usually includes a faraway gaze, they hop down and run off for more play.

All primate infants show similar attachment and separation behavior, whether they are children in the park or baboons on the African plain. The infant who is secure in its attachment is more likely to brave separation.

Many years ago, primatologist Harry Harlow studied infant monkeys under varying separation conditions. Few pictures are as heartrending as Harlow's monkeys raised without mothers, when they are placed with other monkeys for the first time. They hunch cowering, try to cover themselves as if naked, and suck their thumbs.

Living The Paradox

The paradox begins at birth. In order to feel secure, the infant must feel attached to an intimate caregiver, yet at the same time it begins the process of identifying who it is and deciding its self-worth. Bowlby called this process exploration.

To do this, the child must separate. But separateness also pro-
vokes anxiety, causing the child to feel abandoned. This preverbal
state of anxiety, usually well hidden from the conscious mind, can
distort our adult connections as if saying, "I am not worthy of
attachment."

Chodorow says,

> Separateness during this early period threatens not only anxiety
> at possible loss, but the infant's very sense of existence. . . . An
> infant who experiences this anxiety develops instead a 'false self'
> based on reactions to intrusion.

We cannot overestimate the profound influences this period
has on later coping behaviors. As the infant grows, the self becomes even more fragile. Chodorow observes that "Felt dependence increases as real dependence declines." The child at play
runs back to the caregiver for reassurance. Chodorow asks us to
imagine the emotional changes as the child hovers between feeling
part of Mother to feeling *controlled* by Mother. This creates an
ambivalence toward separation.

A recent report showed that institutionalized disturbed children, many from dysfunctional families, who were given a one-
hour massage daily became calmer and more cooperative. Corti-
sone, their stress hormone, decreased.

While touching disturbed children is not recommended by traditional psychiatry, it does appear that these children needed to
be touched.

The Missing Father

Chodorow and others have observed that in many families the
father is "absent," or at least not equal to the mother in parenting
responsibilities.

What effect does this have on the infant? Even in pre-Oedipal
development, the boy has discovered he is the other and begins to
develop his gender identity. The first rule he learns is that masculine is *not* feminine, not mother, and not mothering.

During the separation from mother, the boy-child experiences
another trauma: toilet training. Feminist Constance Perin notes
that boys are less physiologically ready than girls for bowel and

bladder control. Mother must "deal with the crap." Boys are twice as likely to bed-wet. They experience their first shaming from Mother at a precognitive time. This ghost will haunt them the rest of their lives as hidden anger and control/power issues. Imagine the confusion in the two-year-old boy who is experiencing a woman's power at the same time he depends on her unconditional love.

The girl-child learns that she is a smaller counterpart of Mother: feminine is mothering. The girl stays merged with her mother much longer than the boy. He is left to his own investigation of maleness during the Oedipal years when Father is absent.

Many therapists have warned that the mother may use this son of an absent father as a husband-surrogate. Chodorow says, "This [absence] is likely to turn her affection and interest to the next obvious male — her son — and to become particularly seductive toward him." She notes that the absent father is not there to prevent or break up the mother-son boundary confusion.

Father, not being there to mitigate possible incestuous impulses, produces boys who have "not resolved early issues of individuation and the establishment of ego boundaries." In attempting to hang on to a separating son, the mother may cause permanent damage to his adult relationships. Therapist Gus Napier concludes, "Thus, mother and son establish between them the final link in what may become the son's lifelong addiction to a woman's fond, frustrated helpfulness." This eternal boy seeks caretakers among women.

A Sexual Dichotomy

So far we have learned that primary love, the unconditional need for attachment, for human contact, begins before birth. It is associated with intimate cuddling and oral gratification. It becomes sexualized as the sexes individuate differently.

Chodorow observes that most women emerge from this period viewing men as primary erotic objects but less as love objects: "Men tend to remain emotionally secondary," she writes. This attitude toward men will depend on "the mother-daughter relationship, the quality of the father's interaction with his daughter, and the mother-father relationship." Phrased differently, women "develop a *personal* identification with their mother. . . . By contrast, boys develop a *positional* identification with aspects of the masculine role." [My emphasis.]

This gender asymmetry may also prevent men from friendship with other men. It's not what men feel about people, but their social status which determines the relationship. We will explore this difference in the next chapter.

What Does Attachment Drive Have To Do With Loneliness?

Chodorow based her attachment theory on John Bowlby's monumental examination of early childhood development. He observed that the unattached child will go through stages of protest, despair and detachment. Child psychologist Mary Ainsworth related these emotions to infants demonstrating secure-attachment, anxious/ambivalent-attachment and avoidant-attachment. Secure infants had a caregiver who was available and responsive. Anxious/ambivalent infants had an anxious caregiver who was inconsistent in response. Avoidant infants had unresponsive, if not rejecting, caregivers.

Anxious Or Avoidant Adults

Phillip Shaver and his co-workers surveyed a large group of adults and found their sexual relationships could be characterized into the same three groups. Approximately 25 percent classified themselves as avoidant, and nearly 20 percent as anxious/ambivalent. These percentages are similar to the percentages of children in each category. This leaves a little over 50 percent of the adults and children in the secure category.

The question has yet to be tested: Are children with poor attachments going to develop into adults with a similar deficit? My survey suggests the answer is "Yes!" But we can overcome this poor start in our making bonds.

Shaver and his colleague Cindy Hazan reported that both insecure groups of respondents agreed that they were "lonely people" significantly more frequently than the secure group.

The avoidant people, who recalled their mothers as more frequently rejecting, were resigned to their loneliness. Although they recalled their mothers as intrusive and fathers as unfair, the anxious/ambivalent group still retained hope. The secure (less lonely) group reported affectionate relationships between their mother and father.

If the infant cannot respond normally or has not developed its bonding techniques, the mother becomes avoidant. In one study, 81 percent of infants judged avoidant at one year of age were high-risk at birth, showing less brain integrity. Lack of interactive facial expressions of these newborns reflects this deficit and gives negative feedback to the mother.

Responsive infants soon show affective attunement with their mother. This is called "mirroring-echoing," and even the heart rates become the same. Mothers learn to mirror the infant's attachment behavior.

Nearly 50 percent of the adults in the Shaver-Hazan study are *chronically* lonely and lack the self-esteem, attachment skills or attitudes toward others sufficient to break the cycle of failed attachments. For the other 50 percent, loneliness may be a positive emotion.

Shaver and Hazan conclude:

> By adhering to current procedures, loneliness researchers have given loneliness a bad name, associating it with a host of serious-sounding personality deficiencies. Yet transient loneliness may be a perfectly reasonable and functional emotion, like fear, sadness or anger; loneliness motivates healthy people to seek more adequate social relationships.

We may need to seek professional help to learn how to seek friends.

Joyce's Story

Joyce is a 36-year-old editor for a small press. Her broad smile, sparkling eyes and open manner hide a profound chronic loneliness.

"I guess I have always been lonely," she begins. "I grew up in a dysfunctional family even though there was no alcoholism. I'm not an adult child of an alcoholic parent. My mother was constantly depressed, angry, bitter, judgmental . . ." She pauses to reconstruct her childhood.

"I was the youngest by five years, never close to my siblings. I learned to avoid my mother and her constant picking at me. I got the idea I was an awful child . . . but I was good. I never did anything wrong."

Joyce had one of the highest loneliness scores on the questionnaire and admitted every addictive behavior. "I am an alcoholic, but haven't had a drink in six years. I finally asked my therapist to put me in a hospital. I was a six-pack-a-night person. I'd come home from work and drink until I fell into bed. Then I'd wake up at 3:00 A.M. and not be able to sleep."

Joyce admits she is lonely at least once a day. "But that's an improvement," she says, smiling.

"I also used amphetamines — you know that's great with alcohol — and was anorexic and bulimic," she explains. "My early therapy just got me through the week. Now I have gone back to childhood with the help of a new therapist. Those first few years are so important. I can't remember them but I assume something was missing. I was terrified of my mother. She would scream that we kids were killing her and shout she wanted to die. My father was absent, maybe a workaholic, maybe he was avoiding my mother."

Joyce is frankly good-looking with California-blonde hair, blue eyes and a model-like figure. Yet she complains, "Atlanta is as difficult to find a decent man in as Marshfield, Wisconsin. I married a loser when I was 20. I thought I could take care of him. We knew each other for eight weeks. His mother said maybe I could change him."

Joyce left her husband after three years and has lived alone since then. "I always pick men who live out of town or are married. I guess I don't want to get close. I grew up with no interpersonal skills, no ability to read other people's signals. Real intimacy was beyond me. I haven't slept with a man overnight in 12 years."

She pauses, then adds, "I don't know what sexual addiction is, but I know I have wanted a man when I was lonely."

The way Joyce talks about her life, the coping skills which she is developing and her open attitude toward her addictive behaviors bring hope that she will overcome her attachment deficit. She sums up her progress, "Now I am learning how to take in, to accept *from* relationships. I never learned how to receive gifts of things or friendship from others."

Joyce's story and Shaver's avoidant adults bring to mind the image of those cowering mother-deprived monkeys. That Joyce had little positive attachment experience is hardly debatable. She had no one to satisfy her needs for affectionate touching. She learned to cope by trying to stay out of the way and be perfect. She would get what she wanted — touching — by taking care of someone else. She learned that taking in substances could numb the lack of attachment. If, as an adult, she thought she could suck her thumb she would have. She smoked instead.

Harlow listed three "loves" which need expression: mother to infant, infant to mother and between peers. He warned that "Primates either love early or they are apt to hate forever." Self-hate must certainly be part of the hate humans develop. In Joyce's case, therapy may have removed the "forever."

Adolescence

The patterns formed during childhood explode into emotional starbursts during adolescence. Ideally, the individual continues to separate, finds stimulation with his or her peers and builds self-esteem and self-identity. The adolescent will continue the cycle of stimulation and arousal modulation using the coping skills brought from childhood.

Adolescence is a relatively new social construct. In the past, before puberty, the boy was sent to the fields, to apprentice or to school. The girl was kept sequestered at home. The boy was not considered an adult until 25, or later if he was in a profession.

Separation

Adolescent women have a different situation separating from their mothers. Mothers and daughters tend to stay safely merged with one another. Eva Margolies in her book about women's friendships writes:

> While many of us have put the blame on men for keeping women down, we have been barking up the wrong tree. . . . It is out of our emotional ties and identification with Mother that our basic conflict with independence and autonomy is born. And it is with our friendships with each other that this conflict is nurtured, cultivated, perpetuated.

The boy needs help in his separation and integration. Joseph Campbell describes how, in primitive cultures around the world, the boy-child must die and return as an adult. Rites of passage were designed to create the emotional separation from mother into the man's world.

Primatologist Jane Goodall recounts how the adolescent chimpanzee leaves his mother on his own. In spite of rejection, sometimes violent, by the adult males, he eventually ingratiates himself into his male band.

Girls in so-called primitive cultures were initiated into womanhood upon menarche.

Adolescence today is a protracted and diffuse rite of passage emphasizing the emotional pain without experiencing the cultural gain. Mythologies describe heroes journeying through death and resurrection to find a holy grail, a sign, a father, a transformation to a new person. No modern mythology integrates the child into the world of adult responsibility. So adolescents create their own tribes called gangs, cheerleaders, drill teams, fraternities or sororities with different clothes, language and rituals. We pass on defective scripts and incomplete rites of passage to our youth.

My Story

I have another tale to tell of my own, this time to emphasize these scripts and rites of passage. My childhood memories begin with rambling across the fields surrounding Wausau, Wisconsin. As an only child, I played with a gang of boys or with two sisters who lived across the street or alone.

I worked *for* my father in an expanding series of jobs. I pleased my mother by being good and getting good grades in school. However, the major influence on my life was my grandfather. I worked *with* him. Every summer I was his "pard" shadowing him while he did his chores, plowed or mowed his fields and did his "town work" in Missouri. A small boy can learn a lot about human intercourse by watching people of small farming towns converse.

The miller, the blacksmith, the gas station attendant, the bank teller were always acquaintances, sometimes fellow church members and even relatives. Driving down dusty roads and coming across someone plowing a field presented an opportunity for

Granddad to trade conversation — gossip. I could only hunker down and wait patiently while a chew was cut, a stick whittled and tales told. I never doubted that I belonged to the male world even though I could cook, sew and do Grandmother's chores. I learned my friendship scripts in the warm caldron of small communities where everyone knew everyone else.

My first major rite of passage began when my grandfather asked if I wanted to lead the "rick horse" to bring the hay into the hay loft. All morning I led that horse back and forth as the hay dropped into the loft.

After the noon meal, Granddad asked if I wanted to quit. I said no. At the end of the day, in front of the men who had helped, Granddad said, "I'm going to pay you for your work just like I would pay Jack here. You worked all day like a man."

I was a child no longer. I had joined the community of men. Fifty years later I can picture the circle of men, smell the hay and the horses, and glory in the moment.

Loneliness Before Adulthood

Between 5 and 15 percent of elementary school students experience significant social-relationship problems. Many children go through school with few friends or no friends. By the time they are adolescents the figure increases to between 10 and 20 percent.

Adolescents throughout the world experience similar percentages of loneliness. Those in the United States are the highest. About 30 percent of adolescent boys and 20 percent of adolescent girls are "loners" with few or no friends during high school. These students show a lack of self-reported attractiveness, likability, happiness and self-satisfaction. Some students need help in making friends.

How We Learn Friendship

Peer relationships begin with two children determining the boundaries of their interactions. They share information, play and fantasies; but more important, they learn to resolve conflict and to disclose feelings. As they grow older, they gossip. That is, they tell stories about others and through this, resolve what is allowed in their society.

Peer separation in children can cause depressive behavior. Peer playmates develop phase relationships as their heart rates synchronize. This childhood concurrence appears in adulthood as synchrony in speech rhythms and body movement — adult attunement. Such attunement is observed during dating rituals.

Older yet, they begin to play in groups and to differentiate play roles for each sex. Self-disclosure becomes more important and social comparison increases. As adolescents, they continue self-disclosure and gossip, and increase their mutual problem-solving, which includes feedback of the other's thoughts, perceived as "mind reading." Emotional honesty and risk-taking create a solidarity.

If any of these processes are arrested, poor social adjustment is more likely. Most studies on the effects of poor peer socialization have the fault of being retrospective. However, a couple of prospective studies are enlightening.

One group followed fifth-graders rejected by their peers. They were found significantly more likely to drop out, be truant or be in trouble with the law six years later. Another group took the teacher's assessment of peer compatibility and found it predicted a future dropout or trouble with the law or with a job.

Two therapists observed that adolescents who don't have friends need training in pairs to overcome their lack of friendship skills.

Apparently making friendships goes through a series of progressive steps much like developing morality or ethics. Poor childhood experiences can arrest this process before it ever gets started.

Young Adults

The assessments of our relationships with our parents, which we saw in Figure 3.1, take on more significance now that we understand their role in our loneliness. Psychologists Norman Schultz and DeWayne Moore report that "Male and female college undergraduates with controlling or rejecting fathers were lonelier than undergraduates with autonomy-granting and accepting fathers." If the female students had controlling or rejecting mothers, they were lonelier than those with accepting moms.

In addition, loneliness researchers Judith Lobdell and Daniel Perlman found college females were significantly lonelier if there was a lack of positive involvement within the family. Lonely daughters had lonely mothers.

Let us not forget that both male and female college students report that their loneliness needs are met by females, not by males, just as Mother met our infantile attachment and arousal modulation needs.

Mother And Loneliness

Recall in Figure 3.1 how frequently members of the sample said they had poor childhood relationships with their mothers. One of the researchers cited earlier noticed that children of mothers who were less commanding and more agreeable and communicative were more capable of making a new friendship.

I separated my population into those who admitted that they had below-average relations with their mothers during childhood and those who did not. The results shocked me.

Women with poor relations (33 percent of the sample) were significantly more lonely as adults by all test criteria. They also recalled poor peer relationships, which continued into the present. They were more likely to use drugs, seek sex or drink alcohol when they were lonely. Of the 19 women who admitted using drugs when they are lonely, 15 rated their relations with their mothers below average.

Men with poor relations (27 percent of the sample) scored as emotionally lonely and were lonely under more conditions. They were not as likely to have poor peer relationships as the women in the present, but rated them significantly low during childhood, adolescence or young adulthood. They were much more likely to work (65 percent) when they were lonely than men who said they had average or above-average relations with their mothers (41 percent).

When the same sample was tested for those who had poor relations with their fathers as children or as adolescents, but not with their mothers, the only consistent difference was their poor relations with their peers as children. This simply means that there is a strong correlation between people's assessment of their relationship with their mother during childhood and their attachment attitudes now: *Mother influences loneliness, peer relations and coping methods into our adult years. But cause and effect have not been proved.*

Both sexes stumble toward adulthood, sometimes losing or denying their primary support — their parents — either without replacing the support or by clinging to peers, at times very inadequately. Their social relationships with family and friends may be tenuous at best. Both sexes frequently attempt replacement of their family support through sensual/sexual contact primarily with the other sex. Gratification of the person's need for being in touch becomes associated with sexual intercourse. This seems to be the message from our media: film, novel, television, advertising and the like.

Both sexes become confused when they find sexual intimacy does not necessarily supply their need for intimate communication. As adolescent physician Elizabeth McAnarney observes:

> Adolescents need touch to facilitate communication and convey caring. When children are no longer held and comforted by their parents, they may turn to their peers instead. There is almost no data on this, but I wonder if the increase in very young teenage pregnancy comes from the need to be held. They may be using sex for a nonsexual purpose.

On the one hand, Mother may influence an insecurity which seems to be filled by risky behaviors. On the other hand, she might model unconditional love so well that we expect it from our lovers later. "If you love me, you'd know what I want without my asking," is a common expectation in many relationships.

But I am not mother-bashing. Fathers are just as responsible for the dependence on mothers for parenting. The pressures of this society make families an endangered species. Most mothers are doing the best they can or know how. If we have lost the knack of making friends, we have also lost the knack of parenting. We understand what the needs of infants and children are, but we have neither disseminated the skills well enough nor have we sufficient human models to emulate. Modeling parenting in the classroom, as early as kindergarten, is catching on because it successfully reduces classroom violence, decreases the desire for children and early pregnancy and increases parent-child communication.

An Exercise

Sandra had called before the workshop series began to assure herself that people her age would be there. "I get along with older folks; it's people my own age I have trouble with. How many young people are in your workshop?" After the third workshop, when she heard about the role of parents in friendship, Sandra exclaimed, "It's all true . . . everything you said is true. My mother and father are divorced. It was overwhelming . . . too much. I guess I look for my parents in older people."

- Can you remember your lonely times as a child?
- Did they feel the same as the lonely times now?
- Think about the attachments between your parents. How would you describe them?
- How would you describe the attachments between yourself and your parents?
- From whom did you learn your friendship skills?

What Can I Do?

Kay waited to question me after the rest of the attendees had left the workshop. We had been talking about the scripts we learn during our preadult years. She had just returned from working several years in Saudi Arabia and was at the workshop because she had no friends.

She asked, "What can I do to stop playing those scripts over again? I seem to always make the same mistakes with men."

Here are a few helpful hints:

1. Do An Identity Check On The Person

Whom does he or she remind you of? A mother, father, close relative, former authority figure? We expect certain behaviors from people who remind us of others.

At the second workshop, Ed told the members about his important discovery of the first night: "The people were not what I expected before they spoke. I judged them by their looks."

The people to whom we choose to attach are composites of images we have formed of those important adults in our lives. My first wife was a blonde image of my mother. She gave me the touching I had craved from my mother. Women may choose images of their missing fathers.

Are you projecting your anxieties, foibles or behaviors on the other person? When I mentioned this at the workshop, John, a software salesman, stopped the group with a loud, "Ha! Computers are so much more simple than people. I know what to expect from a computer, you know? I expect the same logic from people. No way . . ."

2. Begin Communication Early

Don't assume you understand what someone is saying, especially if it bothers you. Change the words and feedback the message. Tell the person how you are feeling about the message. Express your needs. These messages can all be done in a nonconfrontive manner. If you begin a friendship by "walking on eggs," you are sure to make a scrambled situation sooner or later.

If the person does not like your honesty, he or she is not worth the emotional energy for you to carry the relationship.

3. Let Go Of Childhood Disappointments

Recognize the injury. I, like many men and women, have abandonment fears. Several years ago in a therapy session, I screamed at the person role-playing my mother, "Mom, why did you leave me?" That simple statement brought back many of my childhood experiences when I *thought* she had left me. Then she really *did* leave me when she died. At that time I was trying so hard to be in charge that I didn't get in touch with my feeling of abandonment. That feeling stayed with my relationships with women until I recognized it.

Forgive the individual. Come on, let go of the anger, pain, sadness. It is for you that you must forgive. Yes, there are some behaviors that are unforgivable. If you cannot forgive and you know that it is unhealthy to suppress the feelings by forgetting, then own the frustration. I have a scar which runs from my left knee to my hip. It doesn't hurt after 40 years but it is a constant reminder of a very painful time. Allow the scar to form.

Rewrite the script. Once I discovered that I expected all of my female partners to abandon me, I could see how silly my behavior was. Then I could stop putting them in situations where they would abandon me.

Ask for what you need from your partner. If I have abandonment anxieties, I can let my partner know that a phone call when she is out of town — and even when she is in town — helps.

4. Discover The Feelings Underneath The Behavior

At a workshop a few years ago, a woman shouted angrily at her new husband, "Why do you always leave the toilet seat up at night?"

After the laughter had subsided, with many of the women in the group nodding vigorously, I asked, "How does that make you feel?"

"Mad as hell," she answered.

"Yes, but why?"

"Because it says he doesn't love me. If he loved me, he wouldn't always do it. I've told him a thousand times and he still does it."

"Have you told him how you feel? He knows it makes you angry."

She paused, looked from me to him, and answered, "No."

Don't ask a man how he is feeling and expect an immediate answer. Men are always "okay." Don't tell a man how he should feel. Mom did enough of that. It may take a day or two for him to get in touch with his feelings, but give him time. You might prime him with, "If I were in the situation, I think I would feel . . ." But more on this in a later chapter.

For now, we must begin the job of emptying the heavy load of "uncertainties, prejudices, and frustrated wishes" we carry in our personal knapsacks so that we can "confront the opportunities that are present in each fresh day."

Yes, we have been influenced and shaped by the experiences of childhood, but there is a possibility to learn new behaviors. Melvin Konner emphasizes in *Childhood* that children are *resilient*. We, as adults, are just as psychologically resilient as we are physically resilient. Wounds heal. We *can* change how we are and how we relate to others.

CHAPTER · FOUR

Missed Communication

— ✳ —

*I see communication as a huge
umbrella that covers and affects all that goes
on between human beings. Once a human being
has arrived on this earth, communication is the
largest single factor determining what kinds
of relationships he makes with others and what
happens to him in the world about him. How he
manages his survival, how he develops intimacy,
how productive he is, how he makes sense,
how he connects with his own divinity
— all are largely dependent on his
communication skills.*

— Virginia Satir, *Peoplemaking*

I f personal attachment is the cement which binds society, then communication is the foundation for all solid relationships.

Harriet, a good-looking woman in her 50s, brought her husband to a friendship workshop. Answering the question, "When have you been most lonely?" she wrote, "When sitting in the same room or in the car with my spouse and not being able to get any conversation from him — feeling ignored and uncared for — getting the 'silent treatment.' " She added "sad" and "uncared for" to the words she associated with loneliness.

Although they appear to have a stable relationship, Harriet and her husband Edward typify the miscommunicating couple. Their youngest daughter is entering college. Harriet says she is lonely once or twice a week. Edward says he is lonely once or twice a month.

Edward rated his preadult relationship with his mother far below average. Now, it is even worse. His relationship with his father fares only slightly better. Harriet's relations with her mother were average, but she rated her father a "4" during childhood, "1" during adolescence and "2" during her young adulthood. Her father is deceased now. Edward rates his current peer relationships a "2"; Harriet rates hers a "5."

Their style of communication is gender specific. Harriet expects to keep in touch through conversation. Edward is satisfied with just *being* there. Neither had good relationships with their opposite sex parent. The ghosts we bring to communication with others include these gender differences as well as ethnic and family styles of communication.

Communication can be thought of as a dance form. In those forms where the male leads, planned steps are followed. The male's intentions are transferred to the female by "gentle pressure," as my fifth-grade dance instructor, Mrs. Murphy, admonished.

Another metaphor of male conversation may be found in Greek or Russian dancing. Here, the dancers start in unison, then allow each man a solo turn. Women's conversation may be compared to a Martha Graham dance, in which the dancers tell their stories with their bodies. Women are more interested in staying in touch — making contact — than in showing off individual prowess as the men do.

In any of these examples, when a signal is missed, a dancer may stumble or fall. The flow of information is interrupted.

Two Cultures

How we put words together, body language and gestures can tell other people what we are thinking. But sometimes these methods of communication give mixed messages. We saw in Chapter 1 that words associated with friendship have different meanings and different importance to different people.

In Chapter 3, we discovered that the differences between men and women originate during childhood. This gender difference, at least in part, causes missed communication. Men and women use words differently. Their styles of speaking and even their body language identify them as from separate cultures.

Imagine traveling to a foreign country, even an English-speaking one. In Britain, for example, you would use a slightly different vocabulary: *lift* for elevator, *nappy* for diaper, *swimming costume* for bathing suit. You would also have different meanings for the same words. In England, a bathroom is just that — a place where you take a bath; in the United States, it is much more. Ask for chips and you get French fries.

It is useful to consider the same model of cross-cultural communication between men and women. Churchill described the British and Americans as "two peoples separated by a common language." The same can be said for the sexes. The problem is that we are so much alike, the gender skew which impacts our communication is hardly perceptible.

The Gender Skew

Drury Sherrod said that men's style is separation and individuation and that women's style is connection and social embeddedness. Or, put more briefly, separation versus attachment. The ghosts we bring from childhood include separation from the "other" for the man. He will view women as the other. His identity will depend on his status in his world.

Women desire attachment, but experience men as the distant authority. Her identity will depend on feelings of connection. She will look to women as extensions of her relationship with her mother.

Recently I heard someone say that women knew more about men than men did about women. This may be true. But they know men only in a culture dominated by men. Even if this suppression is changing, women's experience is that of trying to mollify men.

This subtle difference was emphasized for me at a workshop for men and women several years ago. About a dozen men were sitting in an inner circle. The women were listening on the outside. The men were describing quite frankly their "fears and foibles." When each man had his chance, the women were asked to respond. One woman stood, tears glistening on her cheeks, to say, "I had no idea men felt that way. I never knew men were as problematic as we are." Women do not know men as equals. The fault lies on both houses.

Women have learned to get what they want by treating men like little boys. Men even go along with the game. Men treat women as both something more than and something less than equal. Neither has experienced an equal relationship which includes honest communication.

In the last chapter, we saw that a combination of biology and sociology creates the genders. Between ages two and three, the play scenarios of boys and girls become different. Boys tend to frolic in large, hierarchical groups. Girls cluster in egalitarian groups of two or three. Even when the sexes are mixed by teachers for play, the grouping must be maintained or the sexes separate naturally.

Male status begins on the playing field. I remember being nearly the last one chosen for baseball because I was small. But I was chosen early for football because I was quick enough to tackle the ball carrier behind the line. My quickness paid off in high school. I lettered in varsity hockey as the goalie. The school athletic letter is a sign of status. Sadly there are boys who begin their grade school years with a status deficit because of their poor athletic abilities. They face the male hierarchy as lonely left-outs.

Linguist Deborah Tannen says,

> Boys, from the earliest age, learn that they can get what they want — higher status — by displaying superiority. Girls learn that displaying superiority will not get them what they want — affiliation with their peers.

She concludes from her studies that the communication between men and women is best examined cross-culturally. With different goals, men and women are likely to use the same words with some skew in their personal definitions.

Words: What Do You Mean?

In Chapter 1 we saw that women placed "commitment" high in their expectations of all friendships. Men rated their expectation of commitment much lower. However, they rated "complicity" much higher than the women. It may be that women assume complicity in their affiliations while men must be assured of it. On the other hand, women may have learned that commitment is hard to come by, while men assume it without needing verbal confirmation. The different experiences of men and women can slant their vocabularies.

When we examine how men and women rate words in relation to the word "loneliness," we find subtle but significant differences. For example take a look at the six words rated the highest (see Table 4.1 below). The scores and rankings for men and women who are assigned to the Not Lonely group are not very different. Women replaced the men's "desperate" with "desolated."

Table 4.1. Top Words Associated With Loneliness By Men And Women Lonely Once Or Twice A Month Or Less Compared To Men And Women Lonely Once Or Twice A Week Or More With Their Rating 1-7

Men		Women	
94 Not Lonely	65 Lonely	128 Not Lonely	54 Lonely
1. Emptiness 5.9*	Emptiness 6.1	Emptiness 6.1	Emptiness 6.2
2. Depressing 5.4	Isolated 5.6	Depressing 5.4	Painful 5.8
3. Hopelessness 5.1	Depressing 5.5	Isolated 5.3	Isolated 5.8
4. Isolated 5.1	Painful 5.2	Painful 4.8	Depressing 5.7
5. Painful 4.8	Hopelessness 4.8	Desolated 4.8	Desolated 5.2
6. Desperate 4.7	Powerless 4.8	Hopelessness 4.6	Unattached 5.1

*Numbers are the average rating

One word was used significantly differently between the Not Lonely men and women. Men associated "cheerful" with lonely more than women. The only explanation I can offer is that loneliness is associated with drinking "cheers" and cheerful groups of men. It is still the word rated least by all groups.

Lonely men and women were more different in their vocabularies of loneliness. The major difference is their sense of attachment. Lonely men rated "individualistic" and "powerless" significantly higher than the Not Lonely. Lonely women also rated these words significantly higher but they included "painful," "unattached" and "isolated." The last two words are obviously associated with lack of connection. "Powerless" connotes a lack of control. "Individual-istic" is associated with separation.

Style Differences In Communication

There are entire libraries devoted to communication. No one model reflects the many factors and diversity of styles. I choose to use the perspectives of the late Virginia Satir as one way of communicating about communication (see Table 4.2 below).

Satir's "clinical hunch" is that 50 percent of people throughout the world are *placaters;* they are passive in the way they present themselves. *Blamers* make up 30 percent and are aggressive nay-sayers. Satir estimates that 15 percent are *computers,* communica-tion through a shield of information. A half percent are *distracters* acting the fool. Only 4.5 percent hold what she calls *leveling* conversations.

Of course, none of us are Johnny One-Notes all the time; each of us manifests these different communication styles at one time or another.

Table 4.2. Patterns Of Communication

	Four Crippling Ways				Real Leveling
	Placater	Blamer	Computer	Distracter	
Percent	50	30	15	0.5	4.5
Words	agree	disagree	ultra-reasonable	irrelevant	a real response
Body	I am helpless	aggressive, dominant	aloof, withdrawn	out of it	in easy control of self
Feeling	I am worthless	I am lonely, unsuccessful	I feel vulnerable	There is no place for me	I like myself

Our preadult experience will influence our dominant styles of communication. Mom carries the image of the *placater,* keeping peace in the family. Girls will emulate her. Mom may be a *blamer* with the children and a *placater* with Dad. The kids get really mixed messages.

Dad has been the authority figure, the *blamer*, trying to keep in control, cutting people down with "you" messages: *You* dummy, *you* lazy bum, *you* princess . . . Boys will learn from him to be aggressive or to get around aggression by placating or acting the fool. There seems to be one fool in every classroom.

The *computer* controls through intellectualizing. Men enjoy exchanging information on everything from sports and cars to computers and politics. My lunches as a university professor consisted of a table of colleagues playing an escalating game of "ain't it awful." We began with the department and university and finished dessert with "the world situation." The communication atmosphere was negative and I learned little about my colleagues.

The *distracter* acts off-the-wall. Many of us have been in meetings or parties where the flow of conversation has been diverted or stopped by some irrelevant outburst. Sometimes the fool releases the tension so that business can continue. Often attention goes down a side channel, making the business more difficult.

Hidden Messages

What causes the behavior of these "cripples-in-communication"? Satir says it is anxiety. These people are giving double-level messages. She writes:

> For me, the feelings of isolation, helplessness, feeling unloved . . .
> or incompetence comprise the real human evils of this world. Certain kinds of communication will continue this and certain kinds of communication can change it.

Words are not the only form of communication. A person's attitude, self-worth, is also communicated. Some of these messages are listed in Table 4.2.

Healthy Communication

The *leveler* practices healthy communication. First, she must be secure in her own competence. If she has had the experience of many women, of being put down in the family or by men, she can benefit from the help of a supportive group.

Frequently assertiveness in men is seen as aggressiveness in women. But the woman is at an advantage in that she is most likely more in touch with her feelings. She can give an "I" message as part of a real response to a situation.

Men can learn a lot from women's style. Women show that they care about the conversation by their ability to listen and to support the speaker. They also are considerate in allowing an equal exchange rather than hogging the conversation. They add to the information by asking questions out of curiosity rather than by confrontation.

"I" Messages

"I" messages defuse the aggressiveness of the "you" messages we heard as children and continue to encounter. "I" messages take practice. First, the feeling is expressed. "I am feeling . . . frustrated." Then the situation which is causing the emotion is revealed. "I am feeling frustrated because . . . I don't understand what you are saying."

A possible solution may be suggested: "Can you state it differently for me?" Or feeding back the message may work: "I understand that you said . . ."

It may be obvious by now that feeding back the message in your own words can clarify a missed communication.

Intimates In Conflict

The differences in styles, learned during childhood, become quite obvious during young adulthood. College students, when confronted by conflict with a friend, may leave or threaten to leave the relationship; may voice the conflict; may keep quiet, hoping it will go away or just let the relationship die of neglect.

College men who have other friends may not confront a problem with one friend. Those who do not have alternative friendships are more likely to voice their displeasure and try to resolve the issue. This passive retreat is similar to the husband leaving his wife only after he has someone else to take her place.

Women confront a breakdown in friendship if they have a large emotional investment in the relationship but are more likely to escape if they do not. Two researchers conclude that women are much better at expressing and receiving negative feelings than men:

> We suggest that men apparently do not view intense negative affect as an opportunity for closeness, whereas women do. . . . Apparently in their friendships both men and women express negative affect only to the friends they feel closest to. However, women are far more capable of handling negative affect than men.

I wonder if men are re-experiencing their mother's blaming or shaming.

Elements Of Communication

The elements of communication, according to Satir, include body language, values, expectations, sense organs, voice and brain all interacting. Our adult methods of communication are only refinements of our childhood experience. It is not only words which communicate; it is the frame they are in. Let us look briefly at some of these elements which make up the frame.

Body Language

The smile and the handshake begin communication. Even before that, there may be the eye contact "across a crowded room." Desmond Morris and his colleagues have studied the ethnography of gestures around the world. They say,

> Where communication of changing moods and emotional states is concerned, we would go so far as to claim that gestural information is even more important than verbal. Words are good for facts and for ideas, but without gestures, human social life would become a cold and mechanical process.

Remember that the infant learns communication first from body language and facial expressions.

What we observe remains the first step in communication. Is the body open or closed, that is, straight or round shouldered, assertive or stooped? Our clothing industry recognizes the effect of padded shoulders.

Are the woman's legs crossed once or locked at the ankles a second time? Are the man's arms crossed or are his hands in his pockets? Does she interrupt the flow of conversation by lighting a cigarette?

We all have personal space which expands or contracts depending on the familiarity of the participants. We stay away from strangers. We are closer to friends. A new acquaintance can invade our personal space. Men are more likely to do that to women. In a situation where our personal space is invaded necessarily, such as in an elevator, we raise our eyes to the flashing floor indicators.

Gestures may have several meanings, sometimes confusing. For example, the fingers in a "V" may mean victory or an obscentity, depending on the country or the direction in which the palm is facing. We know of obscene gestures which have become fatal to freeway drivers.

Values

In spite of our romantic dreams, most of us associate and partner with people holding the same values. We can't help but communicate these values as relationships progress because we have learned to do this with our childhood friends.

The other person usually infers your set of values unless you are direct with some statement like, "I believe that honesty is the most important thing in a partnership." This is why we tend to choose people who appear familiar to us, who remind us of others we have known. These assumed values present yet another opportunity for missed communication.

Expectations

We explored the expectations of friendship in Chapter 1. There are also expectations of communication. These I call "rules of engagement." Just as the military has protocols for engaging with the enemy or the medical professions have protocols for treatment, we all have rules for engaging in conversation.

The rules of engagement include: the order of speaking, the ethics of interruption and the rites of confrontation.

Men are informational; women are relational. Men try to solve problems one-up; women commiserate and support.

Rules of engagement also have ethnic variations. Films and television give us a sense of diversity in these protocols. Jews or Italians in New York are pictured as interrupting much more than Scotch-Irish Southerners or Swedish Midwesterners. Men have different styles of interrupting from women, according to Tannen. Women interrupt to add to the story by *overlapping;* men change the course of the flow by *countering.*

Even family styles may conflict. One woman described being admonished by the adolescent daughter of her new husband, "We don't do it that way!" The two families were trying to meld into one household. Information shared by one of the families was considered forbidden conversation by the other.

Sense Organs

We now know how important smell is for the infant. Later in life, odor enhances or inhibits social contact. I wonder if our entire economy would collapse if the odor industry couldn't manipulate our anxieties about our natural body odors. For an animal with an acute sense of smell, imagine the aromatic cacophony of odors emitting from one person's hair, mouth, neck, shoulders, underarms and crotch, let alone the mixture rising out of one cocktail party.

Taste is an extension of smell. We do taste others. We use the taste of food at a cocktail party to enhance the conversation. Of course, the ultimate taste is the kiss. How often have you heard the complaint, "Kissing someone who smokes is like licking an ashtray"? Although I *do* wonder who would lick an ashtray.

When To Touch

Communication is being in touch. And we have many different rules for touching. These are often so ambiguous as to be ludicrous. In general, it is okay for a woman to touch a man, but threatening if in the opposite direction.

According to some protocols, a woman initiates touching by subtly touching the man first. Then he must figure out when it is all right to hold hands, to put his arm around her shoulders, then her waist. Missed signals can be disastrous.

Morris points out that where mothers can touch their college-age sons and daughters and where fathers can touch the same children are quite different. Mothers touch their sons less than their daughters on the hair and arms. Can't you hear the boy complain, "Augh, Mom, stop fussing"? Mothers touch their daughters less than their sons on the chest because of the breast taboo.

Fathers touch their sons less than their daughters on the hair, neck and shoulders. In fact, from infancy on, boys are touched less than girls.

When daughters pass into puberty, fathers tend to withdraw their touching. At the same time, the daughter is testing her seductiveness on someone she considers safe. The missed communication can be disastrous for her later relationships. When one prepubescent girl climbed onto her father's lap and said, "Daddy, kiss me like they do in the movies," her father was wise enough to respond, "That is something we save for mommies. I'll give *you* a big hug because I love you."

Voice

But hearing the inflections of voice is just as important as hearing the words themselves. Imagine communication with no affect. No affect is recognized as a symptom of mental illness. Even in the unfamiliar words of foreign speech, we can hear anger, sadness, joy and love.

Consider the amount of communication we experience with silence and distance. Silence is ambivalent. It can mean approval, or it can mean disapproval as Harriet felt. To ignore someone is a powerful form of communication. It is a form of retaliation used by the passive aggressive. How many times have each of us used or been the victim of such nonverbal messages: "I'm not speaking to you," "I'm leaving" or slamming the door? That is losing touch.

Brain

Finally, we take all this input and try to make something coherent of it. *The trouble is that we use experience, usually parent-child experience, to process all these data and make assumptions about present situations.* We give and receive more than just the facts in every message; we communicate *metamessages* too. The *metamessage* is the combination of words and meanings we attribute to the words: the whole image of frame and words.

As an example, consider the experience of therapist Jeffrey Young with lonely clients. Prior to treatment, Young determines to which cluster of loneliness attributes the person belongs. One cluster, called "intimate rejection," centers on the anxiety around abandonment. The person with this attribute concludes that if someone leaves: (a) "There must be something wrong with me"; (b) "If people really care, they have no right to leave me"; (c) "I'm better off being alone than risking being hurt again."

These people avoid potentially intimate relationships. They feel worthless, guilty, bitter, hopeless and emotionally empty. Their forms of communication will express these feelings. They "turn off" any significant contact with others and reinforce the condition. The others misunderstand the metamessage and reinforce the feelings of rejection. The therapist helps the client learn new assumptions and practice new behaviors.

Cross-Sex Communication

As one would expect, communication is much better *within* the gender culture than *between* the two cultures. The same sex has had much more experience with its own gender. Tannen coined the term "genderlect" for the dialect of gender.

Consider here the confusion which arises as one gender views the other. Men bond through aggression and conflict. I spent many hours wrestling and boxing or actually fighting with boys who would become or were my friends. This style develops into adult verbal bantering and put-downs. Tannen observes, "Friendship among men often has a large element of friendly aggression, which women are likely to mistake for the real thing."

All too often, mixed-sex conversations take on the male style of communication. Women are at a decided disadvantage in interrupting, adding information, confronting and supporting. Their style of conversation — particularly supportive — is considered weakness by men. Yet men envy the rapport women seem to have when they are together.

Compare conversation to dancing. Women's dance is one of harmony, community, whispered secrets, gentle touches. Men dance hanging on to each other for stability as they stride and kick. They outdo one another as friendly adversaries. And when they dance with women, throwing them around, they model themselves on Fred Astaire or Mikhail Baryshnikov.

Rock and roll afforded a new form of bodily communication. Men and women dance separately, inventing their own sequence of steps. I have danced with women who were actually dancing alone with themselves, their eyes closed, wide smiles on their faces. They talked to themselves in movement. At times we danced together mirroring our movements. Mirroring is a form of communication we learned first as infants. Mirrored speech feeds back the information we think we hear. Rock and roll is the most egalitarian form of dance . . . and a model for cross-sex communication.

Listening

Mirroring requires listening. Listening is a form of communication at which men are notoriously poor. If status means one-upmanship, men usually listen only long enough to get the drift, then practice what they are going to say next, blocking out the rest of the other's words. Men are instantly poised to solve the problem or quickly react with another story. They do not hear the words, let alone the possible metamessage behind the words.

We do an exercise in the workshops which requires listening. One of a pair is asked to take the role of the interviewer and collect information for a profile of the other using no notes. The interviewee can only answer the questions and not volunteer any information. After about five minutes, the interviewer feeds back the history.

Insights ranged from "I never knew it was so hard to listen" to "I did much better than I expected without notes." Other comments were: "I had a hard time not volunteering, you know, just rambling on." "I thought I would have trouble finding questions to ask, but they just came."

This exercise is especially useful in demonstrating the sex differences in listening skills, and for developing sensitivity for better cross-sex communication.

Ron's Story

The story of Ron, a 47-year-old environmental engineer from West Virginia, illustrates the interaction between words, communication and preadult experience.

Ron associated loneliness with such words as failure, individualistic, anxiety, meaninglessness, uncontrollable, angry, worthless and obsessive, rating them unusually high. His loneliness, as we shall see, is much deeper than missing attachments.

Ron describes his loneliest time as during his divorce period 11 years prior to the interview. "I didn't make love the last year. There was no anger. We separated amicably. It is easier if you part angry."

Ron is about five-foot-nine with a friendly, open face and sandy hair. But somewhere beneath his pleasant facade I had the impression of a sleeping volcano of anger.

"I'm not dating now," Ron confides. "There is no place to position myself. There are no places to find compatible people. The group I identify with gets younger and younger . . ."

Ron has attended personal growth workshops and singles groups for years. He attributes his loneliness to his childhood.

"I'm saturated [with workshops], I've done everything. As far as my parents are concerned, they were good people. But I never saw them touch or show feeling. When I was 39, I started sharing, letting people see who I am . . . I didn't have any role models." Ron pauses, then adds, "I don't remember my parents hugging."

When asked how often he feels lonely, Ron reflects, "About three . . . four times a week. When I'm lonely, I have a tendency to sip booze . . . get mischievous. I have to keep busy. At the end of the marriage I did a lot of munching and put on 25 pounds. Now I masturbate and use a [pornographic] book. I don't use dirty movies. I have an electric blanket. I don't date much. I'm looking forward to my electric blanket this winter."

Ron is existentially lonely. This might not have been identified without an interview. Ron admits that he does not belong or fit in, although he appears on the surface to be very affable. He says he is resigned to his condition, but he remains angry.

Equating loneliness and anger is more common among men who pass from one women to the next or stop dating women altogether. Roger, whom we met in Chapter 2, and Ron are examples. Neither has resolved their anger at their mothers. Roger has admitted his. Ron remains very defensive of his mother. He says he has forgiven her but will not admit what for. He wanted to be angry at his former wife. I suspect that both men blame their mothers for their loneliness — a loneliness caused by their missed communication with women.

Difficulties In Communication

Problems in communication become more understandable if men and women are considered living in two different cultures. Men's communication with other men is based on status. When they communicate with women they use these same skills, but they also are interacting with a culture they have experienced as the "other" since childhood.

Women communicate with each other to connect. When they communicate with men, they expect their style will work. Each culture uses words and styles skewed differently. Add to this body language, previous experiences and setting, and we find a Pandora's box of metamessages at every interaction.

Steps To Resolution

Do you want to resolve missed communication? Sometimes missed communication is not worth the effort — the energy — involved in clarification. Silence may resolve the issue.

Ask yourself: How serious is it? If it requires attention, then you had better set up for success. Provide a win-win scenario.

First, play out the scene with yourself. How will you express your "I" message? What scares you about doing this? Are you ready to listen to the other? What do you know — versus *feel* —

about the friend's behavior? Are there behavior changes acceptable to you or words you would like to hear? Is there a safe place and a good time to raise the issue?

After you consider these preliminaries, ask your friend for a time and place. At your meeting, lead into the confrontation by expressing what you like about your friend. You are taking this emotional risk because you treasure this person as a friend.

Present the "I" message with the feeling, the behavior and the consequence for you. Be prepared to listen and feed back the information and feelings your friend is giving.

Negotiate a behavioral change if necessary. At a future time, check up to see if it is working. If so, give positive reinforcement.

Better Communication

We can communicate better . . .

- By expressing ourselves confidently and clearly. This depends on voice, body language and choice of words and style: framing the message.
- By being in touch with our feelings and expressing them where appropriate.
- By listening well, giving our attention to the other person.
- By supporting the person, if not the message.
- By following the rules of engagement, allowing an equal exchange of messages.
- By sharing experiences rather than dumping information.
- By asking appropriate questions.
- By taking the first step with new acquaintances.

The First Steps In Making A Friend

The first few minutes with a new person are frequently decisive in continuing the interaction. Try this sometime. Treat old friends as if you are meeting them for the first time. Or treat new acquaintances as if they were old friends. See what happens.

Recently I attended a focus group considering household appliance advertising. I found six men sitting in an "L" in the reception area, staring straight ahead, not speaking. I sat in the middle, grabbed a sandwich and asked the man on my right how far he had traveled. He answered, but didn't demonstrate any interest in further conversation.

I continued to munch my sandwich and asked the same question of the man on my left. He seemed more communicative, so I followed up with another question: How long had he lived in Georgia? That opened up conversation until we had to go. The rest of the men just sat there, but I had a great time with the man next to me.

I would have been one of those silent bumps in a row ten years ago. Now I enjoy chats with interesting people by using variations of conversation openers. I am practicing my friendship skills.

Subject	Example
1. Introduce yourself	Hello, I'm . . .
2. Locate	Comment on the surroundings where appropriate, the weather, food, decor, . . .
3. Origins	Are you a native of this area?
4. Work	Do you work in this area?
5. Hobbies and interests	What do you do when you're not working?
6. Travel	Where do you go on vacations?

Just as everyone feels lonely at times, nearly everyone feels conversationally inadequate. If we approach others as interesting people willing to communicate, we will be successful 90 percent of the time. The remainder is not worth our energy.

Questions

- Take a moment to think how you relate with your same sex and the difference when it is the other sex. What changes? What do you talk about? Who "carries" the conversation?
- List some conversation starters that would work for you. Are they different depending on the sex of the other person?
- How do you generally react to confrontation — escape, clam up, overreact?
- What are some of the things you can do to practice your friendship skills?

CHAPTER FIVE

Hidden Scripts

❋

*Well, love is always new, even the
hundredth time around. I said love, not sex.
One can include the other, but the other can exist
alone, unnourished except by physical desire.
Love is a flame that is nourished on all sides from
all directions. Anything or anybody can inspire it.
Sometimes life alone is sufficient. There is holy
love and unholy love. All are legitimate. All are
beseeching the same thing — a response.
And even when there is no response, love can
exist, a tortuous affair, but still a yearning,
a beseeching. Perhaps the case of unrequited love
is just as thrilling and terrifying as mutual love.
I have known all kinds . . . And the language
of love is the most impenetrable of all. It does
not ask to be understood, just to babble.*

— Henry Miller, *Book of Friends*

Jealousy, Homophobia And Lust

The loads we carry in our knapsacks are the assumptions we learned as children. The male culture learned one set about themselves and their connections to the female culture. The female culture learned another set. We have seen in the previous chapters that these assumptions and the scripts they beget can be barriers to making connections.

Jealousy, homophobia and lust are variations on the attachment theme. They arise out of the insecurities we picked up on our way to maturity.

Conspiracy

Men

Anthropologist Melvin Konner concludes in *The Tangled Wing*, "Something happens when men get together in groups. It is not well understood, but it is natural, and it is altogether not very nice."

Men bond through conspiracy. There is no doubt that primate history includes groups of males banded together for hunting, protection, warring, playfulness, carousing and camaraderie. In group activities they easily become a threat to other men, women and even themselves. The only group more threatening than a

93

street gang is a lynch mob, whether of storm troopers, death squads or sheeted Klan. Those individuals have found a place where they belong. Whether they are emotionally manipulated by demagogues makes little difference to them. They are accepted.

The need for males to bond appears inherent in human and primate nature. Speaking of the famous Gombe chimpanzees, C.R. Carpenter reported that after a feast of baboon killed and shared by five males, "A grooming session followed."

Today exclusive men's groups are suspect. They are charged with dominating business and politics. They do psychological and physical violence to women, to children and to the community through their power of collusion. Women and other men are justly anxious of such tight male clusters.

Ralph Ellison described human primates at a smoker in *Invisible Man:* "They were all there — bankers, lawyers, judges, doctors, fire chiefs, teachers, merchants. Even one of the more fashionable pastors." Ellison, the black boy, watches as a naked white woman dances and is blanket-tossed by the men. Finally, he is beaten in a gang fight for the men's amusement and electrically shocked and humiliated by the grotesque assemblage of men.

Yet men appear to need the approval of other men. They need the secret signs and symbols which proclaim that they belong. Men's public image is one of masculinity, virility, competence, independence — a status only other men can bestow.

Tracing through American history, we would observe that as the frontier closed and men moved from farm to factory, their composite image of virility weakened. Exclusive men's clubs increased, the Boy Scouts were formed and sports teams developed in the cities and colleges to combat a wimpy image.

The Masai have a legend of the beginning of time, when men and women were separate. Men raised cattle; women raised antelopes. When the women lost their flocks, they became dependent on men.

Women

The community of women is reputed to be natural also. It has been described as a bond of blood. Women do not have to be assured they are women; they are reminded by their bodies, usually nonsexually. (Men's body reminder is usually sexual.)

Only as women moved from the home to office and factory was their womanliness initially questioned. They were and are asked to behave like men, to succeed in the "man's world." Here their support system of other women diminishes and competition increases.

Valerie, working with another woman, Teri, in sales, found her co-worker distant and her pay raises minimal. She discovered from questioning her manager that Teri had been claiming some of Valerie's sales contacts as her own.

How the sexes usually relate to their sex:

Men	Men	Women	Women
Independence	Adversary	Intimacy	Ally
Problem-solving	Confrontation	Listening	Harmony
Respect	Silence	Liking	Secrets shared
Conflict	Information	Support	Connection

These methods of interacting do not work well between the sexes. When men and women interact in public forums, it is generally the man's way. Women, looking for intimacy in an exchange, are confused by male expressions of independence.

Men attempt to solve a problem while women listen. Women wish to be liked; men to be respected. Men bond through conflict, confrontation and playing the devil's advocate. They share information. Women connect by seeking support and harmony as allies. Men are silent about their secrets; women share theirs.

Sexual Conspiracy

Both sexes see the other sex conspiring against them. Men are sure that women, when together, are telling stories about them. I am assured by women that they are.

In a recent workshop one group of women quickly began to share observations about the gap between what their expectations were of men and the men's actual responses. Next to them, a group of men were discussing the same complaint. They also expected more from women than they *knew* they would get.

Men are sure that women are planning some attack to get around them. How does this feel? I ask women to remember their high school days. How did it feel when they saw a group of girls laughing together and they weren't included? You knew they were talking about you because that is what girls did with girls.

Women in this society feel as if they are in a cultural prison. I ask men to imagine they are in a prison surrounded by people bigger, stronger and meaner. Stepping out of line, being in the wrong place, can lead to attack and rape. Women are victims of this society. They are much less free than men.

The fear of conspiracy is a deeply embedded script which keeps everyone at a distance.

Questions

It has been my experience that men and women behave differently when members of the opposite sex are present. They also report different states of connectedness in their same-sex groups.

- What has been your experience in same-sex and mixed groups?
- Recall films you have seen that showed the violence of men in groups. (Examples: *Platoon, The Magnificent Seven, Straw Dogs, Husbands, The Men's Club.*) How do you react to such portrayals of violence?
- If you played in team sports, what did it feel like to be in a complicit group?
- What is the experience of a women's consciousness-raising group? Are women's connections with each other built at the expense of men-bashing?
- What does it feel like to be excluded from your same-sex group? Is the feeling different from exclusion from the other-sex groups? Can you recall times when you have had these feelings?

The point is that we all long to belong. There are constructive and destructive ways of satisfying this longing.

Jealousy

Webster's definition of *jealousy* is all-encompassing and rich in meaning:

- Intolerance or suspicion of rivalry or unfaithfulness
- Fear of losing another's exclusive devotion

- Hostility toward a rival or one believed to enjoy an advantage
- Vigilant in guarding a possession
- Distrustfully watchful.

Envy And Covetousness

To be more specific, when we desire to have the same advantages enjoyed by our friends or others, we often feel the resentment of *envy*. We are *covetous* when we show a greediness and lack of restraint toward possessing that which others have and we desire.

Many of these feelings can be traced back to unfulfilled desires in childhood. These desires may not have been for material possessions in themselves, but for what those material posessions meant in terms of satisfying emotional attachments.

Recall how we compared our lives, our parents, our possessions to those of our friends. I recall the telephone calls to friends after opening Christmas presents. "What did you get?" "Well, what did you get?"

Years later my daughters did the same thing, visiting down the street to find out what their friends got for Christmas. If these presents represented a measure of affection, attachment or status, then the script was written for future jealousies.

Rick, a family counselor in Columbia, Missouri, recalled a time when a close relationship with his friend Ed distanced and ended. Ed became successful, acquired possessions to demonstrate his success and associated with a new group of successful men. Rick summarized: "We had nothing in common anymore. All he could talk about was his success."

Women's Fear

Women have a legitimate fear of male collusion in dominating society. But this fear precipitates a reactive fear in men. Men perceive women, as a group, attempting to prevent male enclaves in society, and in the same way view women's individual efforts to disrupt male friendships.

One member of a men's support group described his wife's response to his attention to other men: "I'm supposed to be the nurturer and you're getting nurtured somewhere else."

Such jealousy, identical to that felt over "another woman," was expressed by another wife whose husband had been attending a support group twice a month for several years: "All right, you've had your fling, now it's time to come back home."

I heard another story about two men who had been close friends during graduate school but were later separated by jobs and marriages. One friend later divorced and moved to be near his old buddy. His friend's wife began trying to keep the two apart, fearing she would lose her husband.

Professors Gerald Phillips and Lloyd Goodall recognize women's fear of conspiracy:

> Activities such as the weekly bowling match or Kiwanis meeting are often mysteries to wives who often seem unsure of what their husbands are doing when they are out.

Robert Ferrigno, a newsman for *The Sacramento Bee*, echoes, "One difficulty men have in maintaining male friendships, particularly old friendships, is women."

Men's friendships with men decline upon marriage. Finding time for something that appeared so easy to maintain before marriage may be one reason. However, jealousy certainly can contribute.

Tennessee Williams made jealousy a central theme in his play *Cat on a Hot Tin Roof*. Maggie is so jealous of the friendship between her husband, Brick, and his football buddy, Skipper, she demands, "Skipper! Stop lovin' my husband or tell him he's got to let you admit it to him." Skipper's reaction to this confrontation and his death occur before the play starts and are the focus of the hate Brick presses on Maggie and himself. He tells Big Daddy there was nothing sexual between himself and Skipper, "Y'know, I think that Maggie had always felt sort of left out because she and me never got any closer together than two people just get in bed . . ."

As women reach out to one another and experience their sisterhood, they may understand the bonds men try to form. Former Prime Minister Margaret Thatcher confides, "I don't think any woman in power really has a happy life unless she's got a large number of women friends . . . because you sometimes must go and sit down and let down your hair with someone you can trust totally."

Joel Block and Diane Greenberg point out that women can also be jealous of their female friends:

> Pangs of jealousy may be particularly strong in an unattached woman when her friend meets a man. If we look at the dynamics in terms of the mother-daughter relationship, it is easy to understand why a friend's lover can be so threatening. He will bring back feelings of jealousy concerning the original family threesome of mother, father and daughter. Just as the daughter felt abandoned when her mother received her father's attention, so, too, she feels left out of the love triangle when her friend becomes involved with a man.

The ghost of childhood reappears.

Men's Jealousy

Although men may be envious of the accomplishments of other men, their primary jealousy is a form of possessiveness and abandonment anxiety. They claim ownership of their significant other. Hidden beneath the grasp is a clinging to one they fear will abandon them. They experience the same triangle as above, when Dad competed for Mother.

A television docudrama on wife battering depicted a man struggling with his spouse as he tried to keep her from leaving. As he hit her, he screamed, "Don't leave me, please don't leave me." The spouse abuser is likely to have been abused as a child. He may have buried that script so deeply that he doesn't know it is there.

In a similar scenario a man accuses his wife of seeing another man. His primary control issue is to know at every moment where his wife is. Nothing his wife says assures him that she is faithful. The fear is expressed in many Country and Western lyrics.

Men's status includes getting and keeping a woman approved by other men. Usually, a man will not make a pass at his friend's partner. Sometimes, if he determines that something is wrong in the attachment, he may attack.

Valuing Sex Or Love

David Buss from the University of Michigan asked what men and women would find most distressing: their partner having sexual intercourse or a deep emotional involvement with someone else?

Sixty percent of the men said "sexual intercourse" while 85 percent of the women chose "emotional involvement." A man might shout, "Did you sleep with him?" while the woman might cry, "Do you love her?"

Friendships Beyond Twosomes

Men can be jealous of women in groups too. Many men come to support groups because their partners are in consciousness-raising groups or they see women's friendships as ideal. At one men's meeting, a man blurted out, "I don't know what they find to talk and giggle about over the phone for an hour or more."

Both sexes need friendships outside the primary couple. Same-sex and cross-sex friendships prevent the suffocation of exclusive intimacy. These friendships are threatening to an insecure partner.

Many times we bury our feelings, reluctant to explore their sources. But if we allow ourselves to be aware of these feelings, we may be able to reconnect with their earliest appearances — back in childhood — and find the source of our fears. Once light is shed on these feelings, we have the possibility of dispelling them once and for all.

- Can you remember a time when jealousy inhibited or prevented a friendship?
- Did you know what was happening at the time?
- Who was the jealous person?
- How did you feel then and how do you feel about jealousy now?
- How might the barrier of jealousy be overcome?
- How much of the jealousy you have experienced comes from insecurity, a fear of abandonment, a lack of trust? What *evidence* do you have to feel this way?

Preventing jealousy from marring relationships requires an awareness of the feeling. Then one can determine if the fear has any substance. It may be an old script without any merit in the present.

Homophobia

George Weinberg, whose life has been threatened many times while speaking about homosexuality, says, "I would never consider a patient healthy unless he had overcome his prejudice against homosexuality."

Homophobia is the most profound and pervasive of the modern barriers to friendship. It reaches deeply into the psyche and we must take the time to bring the demons to the surface and examine them closely. These demons often separate men from men, women from women and confuse friendship and sex.

My friend Ted and I, traveling together across the United States in 1985, stopped at a beautiful park in southern Missouri for a picnic lunch. A convertible with a man and woman stopped to dump some trash and Ted, doing the same, said to the man, "Nice day." The man looked at him, walked back to the car and said to his companion loud enough for us to hear, "Them faggots is everywhere."

Psychotherapist Weinberg invented the term homophobia in 1967 to describe the "irrational condemnation of homosexuals." It really has several dimensions. The same day as the "faggot" incident, we met with a support group in Columbia. I wanted to hear about men and friendship. About five minutes into the conversation, the subject of homophobia came up.

A man fears that . . .

• He may be homosexual.
• His close friends may be "latent homosexuals."
• Any demonstration of affection will label him homosexual by friends, or worse, by employers.
• To be affectionate with a man is to be feminine.
• Intimacy with a man means loss of power, loss of control.
• To love a person requires or suggests sex.

There is no single reason why this particular society is so violently threatened by homosexuality. The AIDS epidemic has only escalated the homophobia already present. I have been told by gays that they go through the same stages of fear.

Society can control men's tendency for cooperation and bonding by labeling such affection "queer." Society labels its enemies to deny them any humanity. It is much easier to hate commies, pinkos, liberals, slope heads, gooks, chinks, kikes, niggers and faggots than real live men.

Homophobia keeps men in a constant state of alert and anxiety — and apart. I was one of the boys called "fairy, queer, fag" by my peers in high school because I was not a joiner. I know the pain and the power of those words.

Back in Columbia, Missouri, several men at that meeting agreed that homophobia was a barrier to their friendships. Adam reacted vigorously, "I am tired of this homophobia thing. That's all that gets talked about. If you have any guts at all, you talk about it and then get to the important things. Like when we meet again. What's going on in your life. This damn homophobia is a pain in the ass." Silence . . . and then the men roared.

In *Cat on a Hot Tin Roof*, Brick said it to Big Daddy, "Why can't exceptional friendship, *real, real, deep, deep friendship* between two men be respected as something clean and decent without being thought of as . . . fairies?" Tennessee Williams was voicing the hope of many men, no matter what their sexual orientation.

Homosexuality

What, then, is homosexual? According to Weinberg, "To be homosexual is to have an *erotic* preference for members of one's own sex. One may be homosexual for a minute, an hour, a day or a lifetime."

Nearly every boy has had some kind of erotic experience with his peers which he denies for fear of being a "homo." Men behave as if homosexuality is a kind of infectious disease spread by touch. Remember the two friends in Chapter One who had the *courage* to confront their erotic feelings for each other? That is unusual.

A Physiologic Influence

For many years investigators have been trying to find some biologic difference to explain homosexuality. Some researchers reported differences in testosterone levels only to be refuted by others. In 1984 scientists at the State University of New York at Stony Brook discovered a biological correlate to sexual preference in men.

I will not spend time here documenting the evidence for a biological contribution to homosexuality. I recommend those interested to read my chapter on "Biologic Influences on Masculinity" in *The Making of Masculinities*. Sufficient to say here that male homosexuals show a different hormone response mediated by the brain than either male or female heterosexuals. These differences in the brain are probably seen before birth.

Many homosexual men recall feeling different at an early age. Boys judged effeminate as children by parents and psychologists have a 75 percent frequency of being homosexual as adults, according to recent research reported by Richard Green. Twin studies provide the best evidence to date that there is a genetic contribution. Homosexuality has existed in about the same percentage of males throughout time and in every society whether accepting or oppressive of gays. Some cultures, including Native Americans, recognize a third sex.

The Stony Brook investigators were reprimanded in letters to the editor, not on scientific grounds, but social. Is society prepared to accept homosexual men as biologically different or would the report be used to reinforce popular prejudice? The authors responded that, "Many lesbians and gay men have applauded our report of a biological correlate of homosexual orientation. We understand that they see it as an inroad against the vicious attacks [condemning] homosexual orientation as purely willful, sinful and objectionable." The authors suggest that homosexuality may be shown to be a natural variant, like lefthandedness. They observe, "If people are willing to accept that heterosexuality is already determined, why not homosexuality?"

Answer this question honestly yourself: If you knew that the different biology of a person contributed to his or her homosexuality, would it make a difference in your attitude toward homosexuals?

Americans live an irony in which they glorify the leadership of Alexander the Great, Julius Caesar, Lawrence of Arabia, Frederick the Great and Richard the Lion Hearted; they wonder at the art of Leonardo da Vinci, Michelangelo and Tchaikovsky, and they praise the minds of Erasmus, Walt Whitman, Tennessee Williams and Sir Francis Bacon. Yet Americans will not acknowledge that these and many other brilliant, revered men were homosexuals. We view their accomplishments as separate from their sexual humanity and not part of their lives.

The Legacy Of Homophobia

Our homophobia not only keeps men from the support of other men, it also demoralizes and dehumanizes us.

Toby, a young African-American, planned to share a house with two other men after high school. His three younger sisters challenged him, "Why . . . are you queer?"

Reverend James Petty tells the story of a gay couple he had married some years earlier. When one of the partners was dying, the hospital would not permit his mate to visit. Only "family" were allowed in. So the family stood in the intensive care unit and told their son that his heart attack was God's punishment for being homosexual. After the body was taken away, his mate crept in to smell the impression left on the pillow. The nurse said she'd call security if he didn't leave.

John and Chris had been lovers for several years. I met John after he asked for some hospice counseling. While we were having coffee together, he opened up about Chris' AIDS. Chris had been in and out of the hospital and now had pneumonia. During the following weeks I learned how close they had become.

"I never loved anyone until Chris," John confided. He would sit all day by the bedside, talking with, encouraging, caring for or just watching Chris as he slipped in and out of consciousness. I tried to inject some advice into our conversations about preparing for Chris' death. At first, John wouldn't admit the possibility. But Chris' downhill slide confirmed his fears.

I helped conduct a memorial service for Chris. The little apartment was filled with friends, Chris' nurses, food and love. In the weeks following, during John's deep grieving, Chris' mother sued John for Chris' insurance, his employer went bankrupt and fired him, his landlord took his car for a bounced check and he contracted symptoms which could be the first signs of AIDS. Anyone who would say it serves him right as punishment for his choice of companion has no understanding of love at all.

Confusion With Sex And Power

To most men, having friendship with a woman means having sex with her. To some extent, society and both partners expect it. The same perversion of friendship occurs between men.

One evening at our support group, a man emphatically explained to some gays present, "I would like to have homosexuals
as friends but I can't get close because I can't have sex with you.
I'm just not that way." He assumed that gays expected to have sex
with heterosexual men.

Most men do not consider going to bed with a woman an
expression of power. That would be rape, they would think. But
power is a component. And as women take more responsibility
for their bodies as well as other parts of their lives, men are
sensing a loss of their power.

One result of the sex and power relationship is the belief that
one partner in a homosexual couple must be feminine. Men are
deathly afraid of that label. The effeminate image of the limp-
wristed, lisping "queen" does nothing to dispel this fear. Nor does
the association of soft, nurturing attributes with C.G. Jung's *anima*
and hard, assertive traits with the *animus*. Such an association
was not Jung's intention. The so-called masculine and feminine
attributes are not polar but androgynous and can be overdone in
either gender. I have known men so nurturing as to smother the
growth of a child as well as a woman might.

The image of female as a "weak vessel" persists. Weinberg
says, "Boys are taught to do a thousand things a week to emphasize that they are boys, not girls. Most are given to believe that
homosexuality for them would connote girlishness, and thus the
thought of harboring homosexual feelings becomes anathema."

Go to any high school football practice and hear the coaches
call the boys "old ladies, girls, queers, pansies, pussies." The list
seems endless. It is even worse for the boys who don't go out
for varsity sports. They are labeled queer by both peers and
coaching staff.

Michael McGill points out that homophobia affects men's associations with women:

> The fear of homosexuality keeps men from each other. It also
> keeps men from behaving in the intimate, loving ways that women
> would like. There is a fear that not behaving 'like a man' is an
> admission of homosexuality even when that behavior is directed
> toward a woman. Men have a pervasive and powerful sense of
> what a man is, and it excludes a man from being any other way.

Men argue that even if a man desires to be more intimate, more
loving, he will not be, for fear of what it might mean to others.

A woman attending a summer institute where I presented a
workshop confided that when she met me, she thought I might
be gay because I was "interested in men's problems" and my style
was so "nonaggressive."

Lesbians

Women are not immune to homophobia. Dr. Stella Resnick was
quoted in the *San Francisco Chronicle* as saying, "[Women] are afraid
that if they really get close and let themselves love another woman, they will have to have sex with her."

Joanne, a redhead in her late 40s, was asked out to dinner by an
acquaintance. Her reaction upon returning to her male lover was,
"I think she's gay. I got the impression she wanted to date. I'm not
going to call her back."

Marsha, a dark-haired bookstore clerk, spent a few years at-
tracted to women and slept with a few of them. She confided,
"You know lesbians pick on women they believe to be vulnerable.
They call them 'DPs' — Dyke Potential."

Some recognize that there is a wide spectrum of bisexual feelings in between homosexuality and heterosexuality. Our hunger
for belonging can affect our choice of companions. I have known
women who have oscillated between male and female lovers,
trying to find the "right" one. They carried too much childhood
baggage to be successful.

Letty Pogrebin is emphatic on what sex can do to a friendship
between women. "Lesbians? What should we call two women
who have 'an emotional passion with no physical counterpart'?
Nonsexual lesbians? Romantic friends?" The point is that during
the longest war women are much more likely to get their emotional support from other women.

Victoria Vetere, a social psychologist, reports that eight out of
ten lesbians say they were friends before they became lovers. "As
with unattached men and women, I have a problem not with two
women friends becoming lovers but with the fiction that they can

still be 'just friends' after they have sex." As one lesbian told Vetere, "The quickest way to lose a friend is to become [her] lover."

Eva Margolies quotes Dr. Jane Flax, "Making love with another woman can dredge up unconscious memories of the early sense of merging with one's mother. Sexual relations with men are much safer — they're more bounded, much more differentiated. They allow a woman to keep a sense of separation that she might not have with another woman."

And Dr. J. Elizabeth Jeffres concludes that, "In a society as homophobic as ours, a woman must feel very secure about her own identity if she is to enjoy the company of other women."

Luise Eichenbaum and Susie Orbach add:

> Some lesbian women feel that they can maintain a sense of self in their friendships, a sense that may become less clear within their sexual relationships. And yet, as opposed to heterosexual women, often for lesbians the distinctions between friends and lovers are less obviously delineated. For heterosexual women, the division between what we want from men and what we want from women is no longer as clear-cut as it used to be. . . . Women today expect more from their emotional relationships with men. The lines of attachment are blurred as the needs we have in our relationships with men and women have overlapped.

Scripts

Homosexual or heterosexual, our expectations of relationships are poked and pushed by demons we hardly know exist.

It's time to look at some demons. Think back to earlier relationships.

- Can you recall when you have been homophobic, when you have been the victim of homophobia?
- Has homophobia ever prevented a friendship from developing for you? What happened?
- What keeps you from accepting gays and lesbians as part of your society?
- How do you feel when you hug a homosexual of your same sex?
- What are you afraid of?
- Would this fear keep you from hugging a heterosexual friend?

• How do you respond to this scenario? Imagine your best
  friend, someone you have known for many years, has just
  told you he/she is homosexual. What is your immediate reaction? How do you feel deep inside?

Love And Lust

"We have imbued friendly relations with a smear of sexuality,
so that frank platonic enjoyment of a friend for his or her own
sake is becoming well-nigh impossible," wrote Robert Brain.

Find your safe place and imagine this scenario. You are sitting
with your best friend and you say to her/him, "I really love you."
The friend looks you straight in the eye and asks, "What do you
mean?"

What do you say? How do you answer your friend? Did the
question shock you? Are you satisfied with your answer?

The word love is terribly abused in this society. We love (heart
symbol) our pets, our city, our sports team and chocolate. This is
not the same as the love we have for our children or our lovers
or our friends. However, we are supposed to know the difference.

Love is frequently used to describe intimate friendship. The
word "friend" has its origin in Old English meaning "to love
freely." The word "love" comes from Sanskrit *lubh* "to desire,"
through the Latin *lubere* "to please."

The Greeks had words for the different dimensions of love:
eros, *agape*, *philia* and *epithymia*.

Eros

The usual connotation of *eros* is "erotic," the sensual. But that
is only part of its meaning. Eros is the quest for fulfillment. What
fills us may be physical, yet it can also have spiritual qualities.
Remember that the word most frequently associated with loneliness was "emptiness." The spiritual is our way of dealing with
life, filling the existential emptiness. We are filled when our inner
experience resonates with our environment. Music, painting,
sculpture, physical prowess, a breakthrough in creativity can
bring tears to our eyes and a lump in our throat.

Our first experience with eros is the attachment we claim to
our caregiver. It is the touch which fulfills us as much as the milk.

Later it is the conversation as much as the food. All of our senses are involved in filling our nervous system — our brain — with feeling. Yes, we can get erotic over chocolate.

Agape

Our caregiver teaches us to give as well as receive. The love for fellow humans and the love of God for humans is *agape*. Altruism comes out of this caregiving. In being nurtured as a child, we learn to nurture. Our parents teach altruism or deny it. Those non-Jews who rescued Jews during the Holocaust were likely to have been raised in nurturing rather than authoritarian homes. Pearl and Samuel Oliner, authors of *The Roots of Altruism*, found that a variety of friendships was also an important preface to altruism.

Taken to an extreme, caretaking can be a form of control which some call co-dependency. *Agape* expects nothing in return. It is unconditional love. To give of one's self does not mean to lose one's self.

Philia

Philia is the love we experience in friendship. Childhood friendships bloom and die, only to grow again. We pass through developmental stages of friendship, according to therapists Selman and Schultz. In day-care centers and preschools, children are frequently seen grabbing for toys and crying when frustrated. By grade school, they have learned that threats and submission can reduce conflicts. They separate out into leaders — those likely to negotiate and followers — accepting another's leadership.

By the end of the middle school years, they are able to walk in their friend's shoes. Passive friends become more assertive. During high school, collaboration begins. The effects one's behaviors have on the relationship are considered. Finally if the process has not been disrupted, young adults will understand the interdependence of friendships.

Philia is a learned script which can be interrupted before full development. Interdependence is the goal, but it also means fewer and more intense relationships. The result is a network of interdependent friendships within a group rather than from outside the group. Sacrifices are made to maintain the closeness.

Epithymia

The meaning of *epithymia* is sexual desire. Libido. It is the sexual, lustful part of attachment. Sexual arousal can be discovered at an early age, as the child develops curiosity in his/her own body and those of others.

Physical and psychological release is always part of lust. Sometimes lust is all there is in a coupling. But the AIDS epidemic has brought a new emphasis on other kinds of loving to replace gratuitous sex with others.

Epithymia is the hot passion of body parts touching when all the hormones are cascading. It is "making love."

Compounding The Confusion

What feelings are stirred by the words "I love you"? Are you frightened to say these words to a friend or even to a lover? Why?

Friends and lovers share commitment and intimacy in the "triangle of attachment." Professor Keith Davis finds that lovers experience the "passion cluster" of fascination, exclusiveness and sexual desire. Lovers also share the friendship complex listed in Table 1.1: understanding, respect, trust, enjoyment, mutual assistance and acceptance. Our passion for our friends is expressed differently, but old scripts can confuse the varying feelings of *eros*, *agape*, *philia* and *epithymia*.

Homophobia can prevent same-sex friendships from developing because we confuse the feelings of *philia* with the passion of *epithymia*. Men find it difficult to say "I love you" to another man. Ken Kesey, author of *One Flew Over the Cuckoo's Nest*, remarks, "I have no problem with the idea of loving men. I mean, I don't see anything genital or physical about that. I mean, there are a number of men whom I genuinely love, but that doesn't have anything to do with sex. That's a different kind of love."

When the gay man finds a male friend, he may be sexually attracted as well. If his friend is also gay, sex can be a consideration. Several gay men have told me they wished they could have a male friend without sex getting in the way. They find their best friends are frequently women. On the other hand, the heterosexual man finds he is attracted to another man and fears it is erotic, like the two friends dancing together.

Lust keeps men and women from developing cross-sex friendships because we confuse *agape, philia* and *eros* with *epithymia*. Sex is always the ghost at the banquet of cross-sex friendships.

Block and Greenberg report that more married women than single women have male friends. They attribute this to friendships with husband's friends. They also observe that there may be times even in a platonic relationship of long standing when the vulnerability of one or both of the participants may lead to a desire for sex. All they may want or need is nurturing.

The authors quote Janet, a 33-year-old scientist: "Until things are settled, there is always an element of flirtation. If the subject of sex is approached directly by a friend, I'll laugh it off or treat it lightly. Or if my friend is married, I'll make an effort to get to know his wife. But quite honestly, an undercurrent of at least some mutual sexual attraction, unpressured and kept in perspective, is flattering and energizing, something that I find myself looking forward to."

Flirting is fun for both sexes. The flexible boundaries which make it confusing also make it risky — part of the fun. With enough erotic exercise the passionate point is reached where the woman is extremely romantic and the man fully aroused and lustful. Must he prove his masculinity by making love? Must she prove her desirability by having sex?

Here we trip over the dichotomy of sexual intercourse: Is the couple having sex or making love? For many men in my workshops there is a vast difference. Sometimes they make love and sometimes they have sex. And women know the difference quite well. For some women having sex means they will be loved . . . maybe. But for many other men having sex *is* love.

No wonder we have such difficulties. We have different experiences. And we have few if any models of cross-sex friendships. Lillian Rubin found that two-thirds of the women whom men claimed as a friend did not agree that the man was their friend. Those who admitted having intimate male friends judged them as more feminine than most men. Many women find it much safer to have gay friends. I have found several instances where a husband has claimed his wife as his best friend only to find that the feeling was not mutual.

Henry Miller had a hard time separating friend from lover:

> It seems that all through my life women have played a dual role. Usually an affair would begin by our being good friends. Later sex would enter and then there was the devil to pay.

Another dynamic confuses sex and friendship still further. It is what Warren Farrell calls "railroad sex." As boys we learn to hurry a sexual relationship because there is less risk of rejection or the rejection may not hurt as much. The longer the "friendship" with a girl, the more likely the boy will be considered a "nice friend" and not worthy as a sexual partner.

Exercise

Take a sheet of paper for this exercise and write all the things you want from a cross-sex friendship. Now assume you are in a sexual relationship with a person other than this friend. Does this change your expectations of the cross-sex friendship? Why?

Scripts Which Prevent Attachment

Most of us have experienced the collusion of the dominant group. We feel threatened and rejected. The "they" paranoia is real. The unknown "other" frightens.

One of the roots of misogyny may be in men's power anxieties. It is confusing for boys to experience Mother's power at the same time they depend on Mother's unconditional love. They experience women as having great power over their emotions.

We fear abandonment by those close to us. Women fear abandonment and yet are not as emotionally attached to men as men are to women. Men sense that their attachment to the mother figure is also possessiveness — both parties hanging on to the other. Men fear this person will leave or be taken away.

Both sexes — men in particular — fear that affection for a person of the same sex means they are homosexual. The homophobic scripts keep us at arm's distance.

Our confusion in the different dimensions of love comes from mixed-up childhood scripts. Sensual experiences with Mother (and Father) develop into sexual feelings. Cross-sex friendships lead to sexual curiosity. Same-sex friendship feels like homosexuality.

Resolution of these barriers requires rewriting our scripts. The ghosts of childhood need not return as old fears. Our attachment needs (sensuality, nurturing, friends and sex) are what make us so very human.

CHAPTER · SIX

Substitutes
For Belonging

———— ✳ ————

*An addiction exists when a
person's attachment to a sensation, an object
or another person is such as to lessen his
appreciation of and ability to deal with other
things in his environment or in himself, so that
he has become increasingly dependent on
that experience as his only source
of gratification.*

— Stanton Peele,
Love and Addiction

Addictive Attachments

Feeling lonely? Craving some attachment? Wanting to belong and no one there? How do you cope with the pain?

In Chapter 2 we learned that most people seek the company of others when they are lonely. Many others watch television, exercise, read, go shopping or engage in a hundred other activities. These behaviors short-circuit the need.

Some of us also use more risky behaviors to fill the emptiness. We may overeat, overwork, drink alcohol, seek sex or use drugs. *In fact, only 20 of the 184 men and 29 of the 218 women did not use one or more of the risky behaviors when they were lonely.*

I have separated methods of coping with loneliness into two categories — *Addictive Attachments* and *Taking In*.

When we feel lonely, most of us try to fill the void with an activity or "taking something in." The common thread in all of these behaviors is the release of endorphins. Endorphins are part of the attachment feeling in infants and adults. They are also part of the effects of taking in food, alcohol and addictive drugs. The endorphins are present during stress, thrill-seeking and exercise (for example, the familiar "runner's high"). Let us examine some of the familiar ways we cope with, but do not satisfy, our need to belong.

People Addictions

When lonely, men seek people attachment through sex much more frequently than women. Kirk Douglas said in his autobiography, "Sex is a temporary cure for loneliness, a way to hang on to someone, to be close to someone, even for a short time." In a subtle, subconscious way men are attempting to reattach to Mother, who gave them the warm feelings of unconditional love during childhood.

It may be, as Kirk Douglas recognized, that sex is just the most obvious attempt some people make to connect with another. One young women confided during an interview, "I slept around a lot at college. All I wanted was to be held."

Pornography

For this group who seek sex when lonely, human attachment of some kind comes first and, if unsatisfied, is followed by other potentially addictive behaviors. Pornography is a poor substitute for intimacy. Men's pornography fantasizes an ideal woman who will not reject or will initiate connection. This need originates from a man's lack of self-esteem, abandonment anxiety and performance fears.

Women's pornography fantasizes an ideal man who will masterfully and sensitively embrace the woman. Author Warren Farrell points out that 40 percent of all American paperback sales are romance novels read by about 25,000,000 women. Women's magazines which emphasize glamour and beauty contribute to objectification of both sexes: The beautiful woman will attract the right man and be the envy of women.

But men's pornography can become much more objectifying and degrading. When fantasies are acted out, victims are overpowered by the abuser. As poet David Mura points out, the abuser becomes victim of his own addiction:

> When the addict commits an act of abuse, when he is sexual with a child or with a prostitute or a student or an employee, when he has sex with his wife while fantasizing about another woman, the addict believes that using another person as an object will relieve his unhappiness. And for a second that unhappiness is numbed and

forgotten and a rush of excitement does occur. But afterwards the unhappiness returns, the drug has worn off. And the addict becomes angry at the person he has used because that person has not done what he thinks that person should do — take away his unhappiness. He carries that anger to the next act of abuse, to the next person he abuses.

Masturbation

Bernie Zilbergeld cites some earlier work in *Male Sexuality* which concludes: "The urge to masturbate was often aroused by feelings of loneliness." Many have noted that two- to four-year-old boys pull on their penis when they are anxious. One member of a men's group admitted he masturbated after work before his wife came home, a time when he was most lonely. During a similar discussion in a group of women, one blurted out, "'I have to stop using my vibrator." The fantasy in which one is in total control of his or her orgasm competes with the pleasure and possibility of mutual stimulation. This may be why the goal of simultaneous orgasms is so frequently imagined in pornographic literature.

More Than Just Sex

There is more than *epithymia* — lust, desire — involved in these attachments. *Eros* — fulfillment, romance — and *philia* — companionship — are also part of the drive. During childhood we develop fantasies of our future lovers. These fantasies are made from the good and bad images of our parents and from myths of the ideal woman or man fed by the film, television, advertising and pornography industries.

Our fantasies are also built of the experiences we had with our significant caregiver. Shaver says that our experience as children shares a lot with romantic love. For example, both blossom when secure, and turn to fear, distress and depression when not secure. Both work on empathy between the participants. Both are pleasurable when approval and appreciation are expressed.

Remember the anxious/ambivalent children in Chapter 3 who grew up to be lonely? They are likely to be *relationship addicts*, people with unfulfilled or insatiable attachment needs. They suffer from premature attachment. These people grasp, cling and experience mood swings and jealousy. Dorothy Tennov called this behavior complex "limerence" or passionate love. Others have called it infatuation or even "fatal attraction."

Relationship addicts can turn violent if jealous. Fear of abandonment exacerbates their clutching behavior. The spouse-beater recapitulates the violence witnessed during preadult years in an attempt to maintain control. Reconciliation creates the emotions of reattachment to the loved one. Violent mood swings bring the lows and highs of threatened abandonment and reunion, which can easily become established as addiction patterns themselves.

Shaver's avoidant children can become addicted to romance as adults. The person avoids real intimacy by living in a fantasy world. These avoidant lovers are afraid of being close and are unable to accept their partners. The relationship between their parents was characterized as "not affectionate." No real person is going to live up to the avoidant's expectations.

Famous Sex Addicts

Annette Lawson, author of *Adultery*, estimates that about 50 percent of women married after 1970 have had at least one extramarital liaison while only 40 percent of the men in the same period have strayed. Gender roles are changing. Marital fidelity was once considered a value. Now infidelity is only a sign of a failed marriage. Lawson observes, "Whatever [adultery] is, it's lonely, as though each of us has to create a solitary culture from scratch to support our intimate conduct."

It would seem that actors have a propensity for sexual liaisons. John Barrymore was insatiable. He would rent an entire brothel rather than share. Sarah Bernhardt's list of men exceeded 1,000. She declared, "I have been one of the greatest lovers of my century." Howard Hughes employed a detective agency to track down women he had seen in magazines, on television and on the street.

Earlier sex addicts included the poet Lord Byron, who estimated that his 200 different women a year cost him one-half his yearly expenses. James Boswell buried his grief over his mother's death in a brothel. He especially enjoyed having sex in public places, standing up. Philosopher Jean-Jacques Rousseau received a spanking from his teacher when he was a boy. Later in life he mooned female passersby hoping one would spank him.

Kirk Douglas wrote, "Actors are lonely people. Sometimes actors are friends. I envy them." Douglas hinted at a long line of bed partners in his autobiography. At the end of his first "love-madness," as he called it, he said, "From that moment on, I was always frightened of falling in love, because to fall in love meant to become vulnerable, weak, enslaved, helpless. I was determined not to let it happen again." He never found a model of love in his family. His father and mother were separated and he was raised in an all-woman environment.

Colleen Dewhurst explained the actor's dilemma:

> I think relationships in our profession are very difficult. The performer lives in a highly charged world that is often full of loneliness, covered by drinking, peculiar behavior, late hours coming down from that tremendous energy level after the curtain. Actors are uprooted a lot, constantly away from their base of stability. Working out of town, you're in a world that has no reality. Your only reality is the stage, the actual working process. There you must bring forth all the reality within you. And you are constantly in danger, working at the top of that ledge, and coming off that ledge you may sail right out over the void.
>
> You can understand why sometimes people will say, 'Hold me. Just hold me.' Speaking for myself, it's because you feel a need for contact. Nothing sexual — though you can mistake it for sexual. Just contact.

Wilhelm Reich, the high priest of sex, tells of sexual attraction to his mother at age four and one-half, his dalliances with several maids, learning that his mother was unfaithful to his father and her subsequent suicide. He confides that receiving his diploma as doctor of medicine "did not make much of a practical difference. Only my mother's good wishes would have made me happy."

His last words in his first volume are: "Alas, in the end, one always remains alone!"

Commenting on the sexuality of politicians in 1977, the authors of *A Sexual Profile Of Men In Power* report:

These men also make up the bulk of the expensive call girl's clientele, a fact which confirms our finding that the high-pressure demands of a political career do not deplete but rather generate energy, and that a man with the requisite vitality and drive to make it to the top in politics will also lead a more ebullient sex life than the average.

The list of those politicians (and television preachers) caught with their pants down is so long that I would hate to hurt the feelings of those I might leave out. The authors do suggest that these men are stuck in adolescent behaviors of testing their masculinity.

What is the difference between a healthy sex drive and a compulsion? The authors of *Lonely All The Time* say, "For the sex addict, the quest to duplicate this sexual euphoria over and over becomes an obsession. Neglecting or sacrificing jobs, spouse, family and friends, and personal well-being, a sex addict ritualistically sets out to recapture a sexual high again and again." It is likely that these people did not learn the balance between the four loves during childhood.

In fact, to treat this addiction we must return to childhood. Advocate of the co-counseling approach, Harvey Jackins recommends exploring how we learned to associate sex with love. Both have a lot to do with touching. We need to discharge the confusion we learned from the mixed messages, the shaming and embarrassment before adulthood.

Working

While more men than women seek sex when they are lonely, more women than men work when they are lonely. Working is a frequent substitute for seeking friends. This is why I have included working as a risky behavior.

What do John D. Rockefeller, Andrew Mellon, Henry Ford, J. Paul Getty, H.L. Hunt and Howard Hughes have in common? I'll even add Donald Trump, junk-bond crooks Michael Milken and Ivan Boesky and the executives of Drexel Burnham Lambert. They are all "wealth addicts" according to Philip Slater. He says, "Wealth addiction has to do with our attitude toward money." Working is how one satisfies the needs for money, possessions, power, fame and spending. Working can also be lonely and deprive us of our needs for "love, friendship, adventure, physical well-being . . ."

The association of poor relationships with fathers deserves more attention. Psychologist Harry Levinson says males are driven by unresolved rivalry with their fathers. The entrepreneur unconsciously strives to defeat his father and escape control. Women, on the other hand, derive their feelings of creation and nurturing from work. This rather outdated gender difference is melting as women enter a "man's world," where productivity is emphasized over creativity and competition over cooperation.

Both sexes may have learned that one way to get Father's attention was to perform, succeed and stand out. Working gave them appreciation and satisfaction.

Lonely At Work And Working When Lonely

I suspect that men and women have slightly different definitions of "work." Men may view work as a job, as labor of some kind, generally at a workplace. Women may include housework, gardening and volunteer work as "work." But the workplace can also be a lonely place.

Phillip Shaver and colleague Cindy Hazan found that people who self-identified as anxious/ambivalent attempted to satisfy their unmet attachment needs with work. They worried about their performance, preferring to work with others, but felt underappreciated and feared rejection. The avoidant-identified workers wanted to work alone and used work for avoiding friendships or a social life. The 50 percent who identified themselves as secure were more successful in their jobs and worried less about failure or feeling unappreciated. They did not allow work to interfere with friendships, health or vacations. According to this analysis, the more successful worker is not the workaholic.

Workaholics And Their Cousins

One wonders why a business would tolerate, let alone encourage, workaholism? Possibly such businesses are the norm and few organizations have made the effort to increase productivity by decreasing attachment to work. Seen as a pervasive response to men's competition with their fathers, it is not surprising to find aggressive, compulsive, competitive behavior normative.

Computer Addicts

British sociologist Margaret Shotton studied a group of computer users, some of whom self-identify as addicted. As a replacement for human intercourse, these people feel that the computer is much more reliable, much more understandable, its logic is clearer and it responds immediately. Those addicted fit a profile, according to Stotton:

> Their parents were cool and aloof, but encouraging, in the manner of the middle classes, and many dependents did not feel that they had been loved unconditionally. They did not learn the art of loving communication as they had no adequate role models, and humans came to be seen as untrustworthy and unreliable. Their initial needs for human love and acceptance had been strong and normal and many, even as adults, still felt extremely hurt by the lack of outward affection in their childhoods.

Today newspapers report about children addicted to video games.

The Adrenaline Kick

Getting high on the stress, excitement and pressures of work is not uncommon. Philip Slater says, "An addiction is a need that is not only (1) intense and (2) chronic, but also (3) feels as if it were essential to our sense of wholeness. . . . An addiction is something you use to fill what seems to be a lack in yourself." "Cutting it close" gives one an adrenaline pop.

Cardiologist Meyer Friedman, of Type A personality fame, says, "Once the brain gets too much of any hormone — adrenaline, noradrenaline — it gets hooked on it." People living in the fast lane have no time for family, let alone friends. Life becomes one big gamble.

One company advertises itself as "Adrenaline Adventures, Colorado." Their service is a ride in a hot air balloon from which, at about 300 feet, you are offered the opportunity to jump out. Your feet are attached to a bungee cord. Bungee jumping is a growth industry.

Gambling

Some, like Pete Rose, get their adrenaline kick by gambling. Gambling is a $276 billion industry in the United States, half of which is spent at casino table games. Mohawk Indians shoot at each other over the right to have gambling on their reservation. State lotteries are a growth industry brought on by promises of no tax increases. One Florida man admitted stealing money from his employer to support his lottery addiction: about 50 tickets a day.

Dorothy Meyer Gaev, the author of *The Psychology of Loneliness*, reports that Leo Tolstoy's gambling was related to the early loss of his parents. Some sociologists estimate that more than 80 percent of adults and adolescents gamble, an increase over the past two decades. Modern technology — computers and communication — make it easier to gamble. Gambling offers the excitement of risk, a phantom sense of control and the pleasure of immediate gratification. In the workplace, the office pool acts as a social glue, bonding the participants. The fantasy of immediately acquiring "money, possessions, power, fame and spending" — Slater's five addictions — is also a strong stimulant. Twelve-Step programs such as Gamblers Anonymous are available.

Exercise

I have yet to hear of Exercise Anonymous. However, there are exercise addicts. One workshop attendee complained that her male partner was always bicycling. He resented changing his schedule for her. He rode even when sick or injured or when he had the opportunity to travel and visit friends. I told her it sounded like an addiction to me. A recent column by Jane Brody confirms the likely diagnosis. She adds that several million women use "exercise bulimia" to control body weight. They overexercise rather than induce vomiting or take laxatives. They are likely to be asexual due to the resulting changes in hormones. Charles

Levinthal notes a basic instability of self-concept in obligatory runners "as if they were not able to form an enduring or absolute sense of who they are . . . perpetuated by the fear that if one stops, one will cease to exist."

Shopping

Significantly more women (66 percent) than men (40 percent) shopped when lonely. However, men who sought sex or worked when lonely also shopped more frequently.

Therapist Carolyn Wesson says 59,000,000 Americans are addicted to shopping or overspending. She concludes, "Men are not necessarily shoppers, but spenders. . . . They go in, get what they want, and leave."

Shopping and shoplifting may have the same motivations. British psychiatrist Gerald Silverman says that the most prominent features of those who shoplift are marital disharmony, depression and anxiety. Shoplifters don't steal because of need but neediness. The same reason is apparent for those who shop when lonely. Shoplifting may just add the extra surge of adrenaline for the danger of criminal behavior. About 75 percent of shoplifters are between the ages of eighteen and sixty and 56 percent are men. Silverman says, "I would be surprised if there were not a complete degeneration of sexual life in these people."

Christina's Story

A local newspaper carried a story about a 29-year-old public relations director who estimates that she stole $150,000 to $200,000 in merchandise over five years mostly to support her image.

She started shoplifting in college when her family cut her off. "They financially abandoned me," she concluded. So she supported herself by shoplifting. She continued to supply the clothing to dress for success after graduation. She claims the corporations she stole from represent her alcoholic mother who beat her and her father who sexually abused her. Her epiphany came not upon capture for theft but because she was nearly locked up for a serious accident while driving under the influence of alcohol. She justifies her stealing: "What I did has nothing to do with ethics. It was a compulsion, something I had to do." Yet she did stop when she was motivated.

Criminal Behavior

This brings us to the addictive component in criminal behavior. Whether it is the three-piece suit in the board room, the armed robber in the convenience store or the shoplifter in the supermarket, each is a thrill-seeker getting high on danger. Some people sky-dive or hang-glide for the same "buzz." Heat Moon quoted one hang-glider who asked himself before every jump, "Is this the day I die?"

Sociologist Jack Katz sees the same thrill-seeker in street gangs, violent robberies and shoplifting: "Follow vandals and amateur shoplifters as they duck into alleys and dressing rooms and you will be moved by their delight in deviance."

The so-called "T personalities" thrive on cutting life close. They derive their self-identities and their social identities from taking risks if they belong to gangs. The violent robber, like the rapist, gets this thrill from the dominance — the power — over others and the danger involved. Gang "wilding," vandalism, "trashing" and other antisocial activities (sports is a substitute) satisfy needs for self-esteem while providing a self-induced high and a sense of attachment. In biochemical terms, when ACTH pours into our bloodstream, endorphins come right along. Some recent research links the different metabolism of neurotransmitters to thrill-seekers.

Animal Attachments

Pets help us feel good, but attachment to them can get out of control. When a friend was going through the anxiety, anger and depression of a divorce, her therapist recommended that she get a dog. She visited the pound and came back with the classic mutt — somewhere between a large grey rat and a rag-mop. He became the center of her home life, companion and part of her daily routine. Later she had short relationships with other men and women but her dog remained with her through several years of postgraduate work and moves. For her it has been a stabilizing influence on what was otherwise a chaotic existence. A symbol of unconditional love.

Susan, an unmarried workshop attendee, was obviously distraught over the death of a dog she had had for 15 years. She remarked that it was the only living being that ever gave her unconditional love. "My parents never did," she said. "I'm searching for it now."

Both of these women's expectations of relationships have been influenced by their attachments to their pets. I know my friend never got the love she wanted from her mother.

One author estimates that Americans have about 475,000,000 pets, creating a $7.5 billion industry. Fifty percent of the households in the United States have pets. An estimate by the American Humane Association reports 56 million household cats and 54 million household dogs. Often, we feed our pets better than we feed ourselves. We pamper them with special toys, candy and clothing.

Pets have been shown to improve the cardiovascular system of older people. The effects are attributed to attachment between the owner and the animal.

Good Ole Boy comedian Lewis Grizzard was called the loneliest man in the world by one of his wives. His rejoinder was to assure people that he wasn't the loneliest because he had two black Labradors, Catfish and Cornbread, "forgiving and completely nonjudgmental. They are always glad to see me. They care not where I have been, what I have been doing or with whom I have been doing it." In other words, the ideal companions.

- Which of these behaviors have you used when you lacked the company of significant others?
- Why do you think men seek sex or pornography when they are lonely more frequently than women?
- Why do you think men find it more difficult to have close male friends and call on them when they are lonely?
- What does work do for you other than provide an income? How secure do you feel in your job? Where do you want to be working in five to ten years?
- Do you feel forced by your expectations or the expectations of others to work? How does this affect your relationship with your family and friends?

- Are you an adrenaline addict? Do you enjoy the thrill of taking risks?
- What does the phrase "unconditional love" mean to you?

Taking In

As infants, we learned that taking things in — through drinking and eating — along with the associated touch made us feel good.

Shaver has suggested that watching television is a passive "taking in," another form of oral gratification. Of course, we also stuff ourselves with munchies or sip our drinks as couch potatoes.

Alcohol

In *Cat On A Hot Tin Roof* Brick found his peace in a bottle: "This click that I get in my head that makes me peaceful. I got to drink till I get it. It's just a mechanical thing, something like a . . . switch clicking off in my head, turning the hot light off and the cool night on and — all of a sudden there's peace!"

For people like Carl, a workshop participant, the cool night didn't last long enough.

Carl

Carl started abusing alcohol at age 12. "By 15 I was dependent on alcohol and marijuana," he admits. "Over the years I've crashed a few cars, never hurt anyone, but knocked over a few fences, road signs and planters."

Carl is over six feet tall, good looking, the kind of man women look for. He owns his own business and, at age 31, has been alcohol free for seven months. "I tried once with A.A. and they wanted me to believe things about control and power and a god that I couldn't. This time I began attending S.O.S." (Secular Organizations for Sobriety has a 12-Step program similar in basics to A.A. but without the control and Higher Power beliefs.)

After breaking up with Angie, his girlfriend, Carl started going to S.O.S. "We used to drink together a lot. Then Angie went to bed with her boss and it crushed me. She said it was no big deal. She just out and told me and expected me to understand. Now I can't think of anyone else; Angie crosses my mind every hour."

Carl is recovering from two addictions: alcohol and love. But he feels in control of his drinking. "I credit myself. At S.O.S. we build friendships and get a lot of support, but we ourselves take credit for stopping drinking.

"I used to drink to drown out the loneliness, to deal with my emotions. But then I found alcohol made everything worse, magnified the bad feelings."

Carl is still emotionally attached to Angie. "I hear she has stopped drinking. She worked in a bar because she loved booze. I wish I could share this new self-esteem with her. I wish we were going through this together."

In trying to deal with his attachment to Angie, Carl has attended meetings of Love Addicts Anonymous a couple of times and is also involved in a co-dependency workshop. By his own admission, he ranks high in about two-thirds of all the co-dependency traits. He reported that it took him several years to recover from a previous relationship with another woman.

Carl rates his relationship with his father quite low. "He was working all the time, six days a week. Then *maybe* we would do something on Sunday. I think my mother used me as a surrogate husband. That was okay until I became a teenager. Then I rebelled. I had to become one of the rough guys." He still rates his relationship with his father and mother the lowest possible.

Carl's story is not unusual. People drink to feel good. Part of feeling good is the result of endorphin release. There are certain chemicals which can block the binding of endorphins to their receptors, thereby preventing the euphoria of alcohol and the desire to drink. Why don't we employ these chemical blocking agents to prevent alcohol abuse? Besides the side effects that make the cure are as bad as the cause; chemicals do not get to the underlying sources of addiction. If it isn't alcohol, we would seek another behavior to produce the "click" of forgetfulness.

People Who Use Alcohol When They Are Lonely

Women who drink alcohol when lonely watch television much more frequently. They are more likely to be lonely at work, after work and in the evening.

On the other hand, men who use alcohol when lonely are more likely to be lonely on the weekend, in a group and with a significant other.

The Paradigm Of Alcoholism

Alcoholism was the first addiction to be called a disease. Since then, it has served as a model for treatment of other addictive behaviors as well as for understanding the cause of addiction. More than one billion dollars are spent in tax revenues and health insurance a year to treat alcoholism. The National Institute on Drug Abuse estimates that 125,000 people die from alcohol abuse each year. This does not include the approximately 20,000 to 25,000 who are killed in alcohol-related auto accidents or those killed by self or others when one or more had been drinking.

In 1982 before the minimum drinking age was raised in the United States, 61 percent of the 5,381 auto-involved deaths caused by 15- to 20-year-olds were alcohol related. In 1989, 45 percent of the 3,535 deaths were alcohol related in the same age group. Drinking alcohol, "holding your liquor," has been a rite of passage for many children, myself included.

When added to the funds for research and education, alcohol abuse becomes a multibillion-dollar industry equaling the alcohol sales industry. About 330,000,000 gallons of alcohol were consumed last year.

Is alcoholism a disease? Some scientists, including Herbert Fingarette and Stanton Peele, recently began to contest this view. In strict scientific terms, there is no proof that alcoholism is a disease. But calling alcoholism a disease may help in getting research and treatment funds, and also takes away some of the social stigma of being out of control and the individual's responsibility for the behavior.

Evidence exists that some genetic and metabolic factors predispose some people to abuse alcohol consumption. People at higher risk have a different dopamine (the neurotransmitter) metabolism and more frequent behavior problems in general. But alcoholics can control their drinking behavior quite well. The alcoholic is medicating his/her pain, which most frequently is loneliness.

Paul

My father, Paul, died an alcoholic. During my first 18 years of life I did not know he abused alcohol. In fact, he probably controlled his drinking until his environment changed drastically.

Paul managed people very well, was a community leader in Wausau, Wisconsin, belonged to all the right clubs and, as far as I could tell from my distance at boarding school, enjoyed every bit of his life. Then we moved to California, where he acquired and managed a motel on the coast.

In retrospect, I now believe Paul probably started drinking to numb the loneliness. He had left the only social support system he had known for 15 years. From being a community-oriented man, he became chained to a 24-hour-a-day post. Managing a motel is a very boring life, particularly for a 47-year-old man who has felt the reins of power scissor in his hands.

Before I left for college and to start a family of my own, I got hooked into searching for the bottles of vodka stashed in various hiding places. The motel was sold, but not soon enough to change the pattern. Paul was a controlled drinker, becoming perfectly sociable at times, stopping for a week or a month or longer. As soon as my mother had buried her parents, she escaped the marriage by dying of cancer. Paul married an old friend who did not know about his drinking. The marriage was soon annulled.

Paul's sister then came to take care of him. Paul went several months without a drink, but soon became so despondent, he decided he had "nothing to live for" and began slow alcoholic suicide.

The death certificate read: "Lung cancer." One might also attribute the death to 50 years of smoking a pipe and cigars. But I am sure he died of chronic loneliness. Although I urged him, Paul would never come to live with me, his son, and his grandchildren, whom he loved very much.

Alcoholics Anonymous
And Other 12-Step Programs

Alcoholics Anonymous treats the four dimensions of loneliness. I believe A.A. is *one* of several effective interventions in alcohol abuse. It has worked quite well for some people, including a few of my friends and many attendees of my workshops. The 12-Step program presents a different structure for the person who has structured his or her life around alcohol. Issues of power and control are reviewed and reordered.

First, A.A. provides one with an emotional intimate, a buddy or a mentor, one who has been through the same mill.

Second, A.A. presents a highly supportive social group and an opportunity to *belong*. A man who was white-water rafting with his five A.A. buddies was interviewed recently on the television show *48 Hours*. He observed, "No matter where you go, [with A.A.] you've got friends, lots of friends."

Next, A.A. offers a culture with rites, rituals and a clear identity no matter what city or nation one may be in. There are an estimated one and one-half million A.A. members worldwide.

Finally, A.A. provides a spiritual meaning, a "Higher Power" which is intimately involved in the recovery process. Bill Wilson, the founder of A.A., observed that the alcoholic was especially sensitive, "one haunted by a particularly pressing need for transcendence." The alcoholic was chasing the wrong "spirits."

A.A. provides new attachments to replace the old attachments to behaviors which, at one time, numbed one's loneliness. A.A.'s success has prompted models for other 12-Step programs that attempt to intervene in other addictive behaviors.

An Inappropriate Attachment

Paul and Carl used alcohol to numb their loneliness, to cover up their insecurity. Carl discovered that the numbness wears off and the cover is transparent.

As we have seen so far, very few people have single addictions. To isolate alcohol abuse as a separate addiction ignores the basic causes of the behavior. Patrick Carnes in his survey of sexual addiction observes, "It may be that one of the greatest, unacknowledged contributions to recidivism in alcoholism is the failure of treatment programs to treat multiple addictions."

Multiple Addictions

Sharon exemplifies an individual with multiple addictions. Having earned a Ph.D., she earns six figures with a respected consulting firm. Typically, she would arrive home from the airport around nine in the evening, flick on the television and the microwave, pour a generous drink to soothe the jolts of flying and climb into bed. There she would eat and drink herself into oblivion, sometimes waking up to turn off the television or waking up to the 5:00 A.M. alarm, the television still on. Then off she would fly to repeat the cycle.

On weekends she crashed in bed with violent headaches. During a weekday she got high on work, in the evening on alcohol, food and TV, on the weekend she tried making "relationships." When these addictions failed to assuage her deep discontent, she started with A.A. — graduating to Overeaters Anonymous and Co-dependents Anonymous. Now she attends four or five 12-Step programs a week.

Sharon is not unusual. She fits the criteria of lonely people with poorly developed social skills. Sharon rates her relationships with her parents, particularly with her father, as awful. She has never felt accepted by her father, even with her six-figure salary.

Twelve-step programs provide acceptance, the only condition being that the participants accept the structure in return. The alcoholic's total dependence on alcohol abuse is not replaced in A.A. by total independence, but by conditional dependence on the process.

Enabling Abusive Attachments

Our society trains us to numb the pain of loneliness, and awareness of existential "aloneness." Most of us have grown up seeing our role models use alcohol, caffeine, nicotine and, for some, controlled substances as part of the rites of passage to adulthood. One report estimates that alcohol was depicted or alluded to about 7.5 times per hour of prime-time television. In fact, television — our major addiction, the medium we turn to the most when lonely — repeats the message that drugs make us feel good. That we should expect immediate gratification in every facet of our lives.

Our culture enables the drinker by making relatively cheap alcohol easily available. A convivial society based on the consumption of alcohol among friends in neighborhood "Cheers" bars often creates a setting for abuse.

James Schaeffer, studying Country and Western bars, reported, "Hard drinkers prefer listening to slow paced, wailing, lonesome, self-pitying music, generally during slow times at the bar scene." Country and Western music with its emphasis on loving and leaving (or flirtin' and hurtin') is the epitome of attachment problems drowned in alcohol.

Hank Williams, Sr., best represents the genre. His songs plead for attachment and bemoan the lack of it: "I've Got The Lovesick Blues," "Cold, Cold Heart," "If You Loved Me Half As Much As I Love You," "Alone and Foresaken," "Long Gone Lonesome Blues" and "Nobody's Lonesome for Me." Williams died alone in the back of his Cadillac, somewhere between Tennessee and West Virginia of a combination of alcohol, chloral hydrate, barbituate and amphetamine overdose.

Williams' addictive life began early. His father left for a veterans hospital when he was seven. His mother was described as "strong, controlling." The effect on Hank was that he "never felt an adequate male." This "thin, lonesome sort of boy" probably started on moonshine at age eleven. His colleague, Frank Price, observed, "I think he drank because he wanted people to pay attention to him. He wanted people to show him they loved him, and this was his way of testing them." A therapist would call it acting out.

Famous Women Alcoholics

The roots of substance abuse begin early in the lives of many of the famous. Consider some of our female idols. Teen movie star Drew Barrymore has led a life of substance abuse sufficient to warrant two autobiographies already. This most recent member of a long line of theatrical dypsomaniacs began her alcoholism at age nine, but she added tobacco, cocaine and marijuana use before receiving treatment five years later — at 14!

Examining Drew Barrymore's genetic heritage, one might expect her to be an alcoholic. Her father, John Drew, Aunt Diana, Grandfather John, Great-uncle Lionel, Great-aunt Ethel and Great-grandfather Maurice were all alcoholics. But there were other circumstances. Her mother, Jaid, left her father before Drew was born and she hasn't seen him for many years. Her mother enabled her alcohol use through lax parenting and control issues around her career. Drew began running with the fast drug crowd by the age of seven.

Drew's first cure came two years after Lucy Barry Robe documented the alcoholism of more than 160 women celebrities in *Co-starring Famous Women and Alcohol.* The purpose of the book was to remove the stigma of women as alcoholics and show that alcoholism is a treatable disease.

Robe quotes Marilyn Monroe: "Sometimes I think the only people who stay with me and really listen are people I hire. . . . Why can't I have friends . . . who want nothing from me?"

Entertainment is frequently a lonely profession. Susan Hayward complained, "You aim for all the things you've been told stardom means — the rich life, the applause, the parties cluttered with celebrities, the awards. Then it is nothing, really nothing. It is like a drug that lasts just a few hours, a sleeping pill. When it wears off, you have to live without its help."

Drugs

"She [Helen] threw into the wine which they were drinking a drug which takes away grief and passion and brings forgetfulness of all ills." — Homer, *The Odyssey*

I started smoking, really smoking, not just sneaking cigarettes from my parents, at age 12. Then, as today, buying "fags" was easy, and huddling over a cup of "java" was an early ritual in hanging out in the little cafes. Boy-bonding began with sharing "cigs" and coffee money as well as stories. My first roaring drunk was on champagne stolen from a wedding. When I was sent to a boys' boarding school at age 13, the ritual of sneaking smokes and alcohol was solidified because it was proscribed. Risking demerits or suspension made the vice much more pleasurable. Thrill-seeking is taught early in our culture. Rites of passage included smoking privileges as a senior.

Entrance Drugs

It is important to emphasize that the beginnings of drug abuse reach down into childhood and drug socialization. But even if that were not the case, our order of priorities for drug abuse should begin where it is costing us the most. Our first priority should be nicotine.

Nicotine

The figures are soft, but the relationship is consistent: Somewhere between 346,000 and 390,000 people die of tobacco abuse each year. Compare this to the estimated number of people who die of cocaine abuse — between 2,000 and 3,000. The Secretary of Health recently reported that smoking costs the country more than 52 billion dollars annually in healthcare and lost productivity. This compares to the estimated 100 billion dollars and 50,000 deaths air pollution costs each year.

Nicotine looks and acts like the neurotransmitter acetylcholine. It releases an avalanche of neuropeptides in our blood: vasopressin (increasing the heart rate and blood pressure), growth hormone, prolactin, ACTH (causing adrenal corticoid release) and beta-endorphin. While the body's physiology is getting a jump-start, the endorphin release reduces any associated anxiety. Authors Harvey Milkman and Stanley Sunderworth conclude, "Growing up consists of finding the right substitutes for your thumb." Smoking tobacco is one form of thumb-sucking.

However, psychiatrists are complaining that removing cigarettes from psychiatric institutions will keep patients more depressed. Has nicotine been treating our national depression, loneliness? Researchers have used the anti-anxiety drug buspirone to reduce the irritability, restlessness, hunger, sadness and lack of concentration in smokers during withdrawal of nicotine.

Caffeine

Researcher Kathryn Grahm recently found that people abuse alcohol for the same reason they consume caffeine: "Personal effects." Linking the buzz of alcohol with the altered states produced by other addictive drugs and behaviors is not unreasonable. Drinking four or more cups of coffee a day increases the risk of heart attack by about 40 percent. The famous French author Balzac drank more than 50 cups a day and actually died from caffeine poisoning.

Does this seem familiar to you? One morning as I was driving, I was forced to brake when a Ford Escort suddenly pulled out in front of me. Following behind this morning risk-taker, I saw he was dressed in a business suit, drove with his right hand while alternately pulling drags on a cigarette and managing a coffee cup. The two and one-half cups of coffee he will probably consume before getting down to business at work will double the level of epinephrine (adrenaline) in his blood. Pumped up with nicotine and caffeine, he's now wired for the day. If not, he can control his high by frequent refueling. At day's end he will come down with alcohol or other sedatives while still sucking on his surrogate thumb. Research has shown that heavy smoking can also contribute to impotency in men. Eighty percent of impotent men are heavy smokers.

Precedents For Drug Abuse

The first three predictors for cocaine use in adolescents are cigarette and marijuana smoking and truancy from school. Researchers interviewed a group of seventh, eighth and ninth graders. Only a few years later in a follow-up interview, the middle school students (now in high school) who admitted intending to use drugs showed increased drug use, particularly cigarettes and hard drugs. They predicted abuse of drugs in middle school and fulfilled the prophecy in high school. The authors observed that the kind of family setting contributed heavily to drug use.

It is difficult to focus on the real impact of drug addiction in the United States. The National Institute on Drug Abuse estimates about 4,000 deaths a year due to heroin/morphine abuse, 2,000 due to cocaine and 75 due to marijuana. Compare these numbers to the 346,000 deaths attributed to tobacco use each year.

We cannot ignore the fact that tobacco appears to be the entry drug to other abuse. Peele reports that "smokers have the highest rates of car accidents and traffic violations, and are more likely to drink when they drive." He quotes R.R. Clayton who says that the heroin user is preaddicted to tobacco and alcohol. One need only to attend treatment groups for drug and/or alcohol abuse and find the rooms blue with choking smoke.

Cindy And Her Father

This is Cindy's story: "I was eighteen when my father left my mother. He was psychologically abusive, always putting down my mom. We would have these beautiful dinners with the family gathered all around and he would abuse my mom. I did a lot of wild things growing up. I should be dead. Drugs and sex. Come to think of it, I had a pretty messed up childhood, too."

Cindy is in her late 20s. She wears her auburn hair long, falling on her shoulders. She has moved away from her family in the north to be on her own. She admits she has been lonely daily since her move. Her boyfriend is a cocaine middle man and at the time of the interview she volunteered she hadn't had any drugs for a week. "I want to leave the guy, but I can't. He sweet-talks me back."

She returns to talking about her parents. "When Mom and Dad divorced, Mom went back to school, upgraded her degree and really became her own person. Then they started dating again. It looked real cute. But just as soon as they remarried, they fell back into their old habits. I'm ashamed of my mother. I guess she is afraid no one will take care of her when she gets older."

Cindy has no trouble attaching to men in the fast crowd who take her out, show her a good time and ignore her until they want her again. "I guess I like the excitement."

She describes a recent experience with her boyfriend when she thought he was involved with another woman. "I was sick and Richard was supposed to come by at 10:30 PM. I waited, but he didn't show up. At midnight, half-worried, half-angry, I called his house. A woman answered the phone, but I hung up without speaking. After that, I couldn't sleep at all, so I got up, got dressed and drove over to his house. No one was home. Finally, he called with a story about being abducted by his friends. I think I'm in control of these relationships until I turn into putty."

Cindy is addicted to "living on the edge." She admits that at times she has been addicted to alcohol, binge-eating, drugs and sexual attachments. Surviving some close calls as a young adult has led her to believe she can cope with anything. I've asked Cindy if while growing up, she had a positive role model. Her answers are vague as if she can't understand the question. "I used to envy my girlfriends for their normal parents, but they were always complaining, too. I don't know . . . I just don't know."

Cocaine has not always been the object of a massive governmental crackdown. Victorian actress Sarah Bernhardt used cocaine. Coca-Cola removed cocaine from its original formula in 1903. The 60 milligram, eight-ounce serving was equal to a modern intranasal dose. Caffeine is still present in many soft drinks. It is worth noting that cocaine is just another "speed," different from the 26-year amphetamine addiction of Kitty Dukakis or from the schizophrenia-like PCP (phencyclidine) induced behavior only in degree, not in kind.

Eating: Filling The Empty Space

Eating is a substitute for true intimacy and risk. If we want to change our bodies, we have to change our relationships. . . . Food is that single, solitary, lonely substance that is ever ready and never fails."

Judi Hollis, *Fat Is A Family Affair*

Maria's Story

I watch Maria sip on a soft drink as she sits across from me in the school cafeteria. Maria is a 21-year-old with dark hair. She complains she has problems with relationships with men. "I grab on and smother them. My former boyfriend said he wasn't surprised when I told him I had attempted suicide. He said I was crazy."

Maria is quite smart but finds she can't study because, she says, she can't concentrate. After her first suicide attempt, she considered slashing her wrists again while attending college. She attended an Overeaters Anonymous group but found the members of that particular group too old. She is now attending an Al-Anon group and feels quite at home.

Maria said she was addicted to long-distance running until it hurt her body. "I don't exercise anymore," she confides. "When I used to come home late at night from work at the movie theater, I would stop by the grocery store and load up with junk food. Then I would go to my room, turn on the TV and stuff myself. Once I got full, I would either fall asleep or go purge."

I asked Maria if vomiting felt good. "Yeah, I guess so. It made me fall asleep."

According to Dr. Darryl Neill, "It appears that the vomiting in bulimia, being stressful, triggers a bodily response which brings about the release of endorphins and enkephalins, so it may be that the addiction is being maintained by the chemical release of pleasure transmitted in the nervous system."

Maria continues, "My folks were asleep. I'd sleep all morning until they went out. I never saw them.

"One night after work I took my brother's razor blade and my mother's allergy pills. I started taking them and I got scared and called a friend at work. She came right over and we went to an emergency clinic nearby. But they sent us to the hospital. They pumped my stomach because they couldn't get me to throw up. Imagine that!

"Have you ever had your stomach pumped? They stick a large tube down your nose. It makes you gag, makes your throat raw — I had to drink charcoal — then they pump you out.

"I called my mom from the hospital without mentioning where I was. But she already knew. The emergency clinic had called her. When I got home, my mother asked me where I had been. I lied to her, but she told me she already knew. She wanted to get me with a shrink.

"The next night my parents pulled me out of work, saying they were taking me to the shrink. But when we got to the clinic, they walked me right past the psychiatrist's door. Then I knew they were committing me. I had to agree to sign self-commitment papers.

"I have to admit it was the best thing for me. Oh, it was hell at first, but it really helped me."

Maria explained that her mother, who is not her biological parent, has been a recovering alcoholic for eight years. "My mother's father is also an alcoholic and she used to care for him. I don't know if there is any alcoholism in my biological family. I wonder about my natural mother and father. Are they depressed or happy? Do their families have any genetic diseases?"

Maria rates her relationship with her mother "poor" as a child and "very poor" as an adolescent. Her relationship with her father remains very poor.

"I was six weeks old when they adopted me. Mother says I screamed when she tried to touch me. I guess I was a problem baby and we never really bonded.

"When I was ten or eleven, I realized my parents were having marriage problems. They are divorcing now. In the past few months, I've become friends with my mother. But I still have some issues with my father."

Maria's honesty was touching. In a later interview I learned that she was curious about having a lesbian relationship with her roommate and was seeking counseling help because she thought she was bisexual.

Why Eat?

The authors of *The Paleolithic Prescription* define obesity as a weight 20 percent or more above the insurance tables. This criterion may still be less satisfactory than what was healthy for our ancestors. By today's standards ". . . about 30 percent of American men and 20 percent of American women between the ages of 30 and 60 are obese."

Following the "paleolithic" description, we would expect many more overweight people. Due to the more concentrated calories of American food — high in saturated fat — three pounds of today's food is sufficient to supply our needed calories. Five pounds of the paleolithic diet was necessary to supply the diet of our gathering and hunting ancestors.

But do these three pounds satisfy us physiologically or do we still feel empty? Hunger is a very complicated physiological and psychological phenomenon. Therapist Judi Hollis, at one time weighing 222 pounds herself, says that besides nourishment we get appreciation, security, relaxation, sex and emotional release from eating.

Three general categories of eating disorders are worth considering for their relationship to loneliness and addictive behaviors: obesity, anorexia and bulimia. More men than women are obese, but many more women than men are anorexic or bulimic.

Obesity

Most likely, there are multiple causes of obesity. Endocrine imbalance as the major factor is quite rare. There is, however, a genetic component which places some people more at risk. The Pima Indians of Arizona have an inherited form of obesity. Two-thirds of obese people have at least one obese parent and one-fourth have two. On the other hand, if both parents are thin, the chance of being obese is one out of ten.

Obesity involves two variables: too many fat cells and fat-engorged fat cells. During the first two years of life the number of fat cells increases, as they will again just prior to puberty. Overfeeding at this time increases the number of fat cells even more than would normally take place. An excess of calories is stored in the fat cells. The major culprit in American obesity is too much fat in our diets.

Mainland Chinese actually eat 20 percent more calories than Americans when body size is taken into account. Americans derive 70 percent of their protein from animal sources (heavily marbled with fat) while Chinese obtain only seven percent from animals. The fat which Americans eat is much more frequently saturated (the bad kind, hard like butter), rather than polyunsaturated (the good kind, liquid like safflower oil).

Anorexia And Bulimia

Anorexia and bulimia are sometimes considered two sides of the same coin. While the anorexic attempts to keep something out, the bulimic tries to take something in, then to get rid of it. However, there is great overlap in their psychology and behavior. Bulimic behavior may begin after an episode of drastic dieting. Anorexia is diagnosed by a body weight at least 25 pounds below the expected norm and the absence of body fat. Bulimia is diagnosed by binge-eating behavior usually of high calorie foods, a feeling of being out of control and at least two episodes per week of vomiting and/or laxative use over a three-month period.

Joan Jacobs Brumberg classifies anorexia as a disease of affluent society. Many patients are well-educated, Caucasian females, 15 to 25 years old, middle- to upper-class, in westernized countries. Brumberg says, "The human appetite is unequivocally misused in the service of a multitude of nonnutritional needs. As a result, both anorexia nervosa and obesity are characteristic of modern life and will continue to remain so. Sadly, the cult of diet and exercise is the closest thing our secular society offers women in terms of a coherent philosophy of the self." Brumberg says the personal ambition to "do it all" by today's women requires a drive and compulsion similar to the anorexic's.

Judi Hollis compares the psychological experiences of teenage anorexics to those of 40-year-old male runners. Both may be getting pleasure from their endorphins.

Parents

Anorexics and bulimics have opposite feelings about their parental relationships. Anorexics describe their mothers as domineering, intrusive, overprotective and discouraging separation.

As an infant, the future anorexic's signals for nutritional needs may have been misread, resulting in inappropriate behavior patterns. One example is refusing to feed on demand and bouncing instead. The adolescent, seeing herself become "like Mother" (including menstruation), tries to separate and at the same time remain childlike. Borderline patients with affective disorders, who are anorexic, experience the parental overinvolvement as *malevolently* intrusive. They feel enmeshed, trapped and paranoid. Those less affective as a child became a "parent pleaser" and later fear abandonment.

Bulimics, on the other hand, experience their parents as under-involved. Mothers are perceived as passive, rejecting, disengaged and emotionally unavailable.

As children, the future bulimics learn that food can also be a satisfying attachment object. They suffer large mood swings, have suicidal thoughts and show impulsive behavior including self-mutilation, sexual acting out and substance abuse (61 percent alcohol and 46 percent drugs).

There is a higher incidence of affective disorders and alcohol-ism among relatives of bulimics (53 percent have first degree relatives with major affective disorders) than in anorexia. Major initiating factors include dieting (59 percent), family problems (58 pecent), teasing about appearance (56 percent), problems in ro-mantic relationships (55 percent), leaving home (42 percent) and failure at school or work (42 percent).

While relationships with Mother are emphasized in the above studies, only 37 percent of our sample rated their maternal relationships as poor. However, 67 percent said their relation-ships with their fathers were poor. Clinical psychologist Margo Maine associates fathers with eating disorders. She observes, "We have excused fathers from our thinking about what helps children to grow up and what hurts them in the process." We recognized in Chapter 3 the importance of the father in helping the girl-child separate from her mother and in supplying a pos-itive male image.

We need to look at the brain as well as the environment in which it grows. A highly significant percentage of bulimics (67 percent) show positive tests for depression and hypothalamus dysfunction.

Mira Dana, author of *Fed Up and Hungry*, observed,

> In our work with bulimic women we have come across women who are very isolated, with no friends and no close relationships, who feel both unwilling and unable to create such relationships. At the other extreme is the bulimic woman who has many friends, many relationships, is much appreciated and well liked. At both of these extremes, the woman feels a sense of isolation and intense loneliness, a feeling of being a fraud and unreal.

A Disease Of Civilization

The fat-saturated American diets may be damaging to our health by inducing rapid growth in our children. This is associated with increased risk of cancer of the reproductive organs and the breast in later years. Our "good" nutrition causes menstruation three to six years earlier than the Chinese. We beget girls whose physical development far outpaces their cognitive development. As Konner says, their ability to understand the consequences of their actions lags behind their ability to make babies. One mother who got pregnant as a 16-year-old high school sophomore recalled in a television interview, "I didn't have a lot in my life. All of my friends were having babies. I wanted one, too."

Fat reduction is a $33 billion-a-year industry making claims which cannot be fulfilled. Unknown as yet is whether each person has a "set weight" from which any large deviation causes increased or decreased caloric intake. Such a set weight could contribute to the roller-coaster effect of dieting and subsequent weight gain. Is this set weight influenced genetically or biologically? After birth or both before and after? How deeply are we influenced by social expectations and advertising to change our body images and determine how much and what we eat? If so, how? The role of endorphins is paradoxical; they can cause hunger and satisfy hunger.

Endorphins And Hunger

The hungry time in animals comes when the endorphin levels are the highest and the animals are least sensitive to pain. Opioid antagonists reduce feeding behavior by producing a feeling of satiety (fullness). Endorphin release and endorphin receptors might be food specific (fat, protein, carbohydrate). That is, one food group might produce satiety better than another.

Naltrexone, which prevents endorphin action, reduces sugar liking in humans. Sugar increases the effectiveness of the endorphins, causes release of endorphins and serotonin and reduces sensitivity to pain. Eating for some may be a way to numb physical pain. Individual Americans consume on the average of 100 pounds of sugar per year.

Food deprivation, stress and intake of enjoyable foods all stimulate the endogenous opioid system.

No doubt attachment anxiety contributes to obesity. One member of a support group confided, "When my wife leaves, I go crazy. I can't stop eating. Going shopping . . . if I buy a pie, I can't keep it a week. I'll eat it in one night."

Another man added, "When Claire was gone, I used to eat, too. But I'm tired of being anxious over waiting for females." This man and two others in the group of six admitted addiction to women. One of these men sought women while traveling in the Far East. This man appeared within his weight range; the other two were at least 20 pounds too heavy.

Oprah Winfrey had an epiphany one night over her food addiction. "I realized it was because I wasn't getting the attention I wanted and it was making me feel anxious. That's when I realized it was a pattern. I saw that when I had any kind of anxiety in my life, I would instantly want to eat. All those years when I said, 'I'm just eating because I like food.' All those years when I said, 'I never have stress in my life. I don't know what stress is!' I didn't have it because I blocked the stress by eating."

How Taking In Makes Us Feel Good

The simple conclusion is that we take things into our bodies because it makes us feel good. We feel good because our internal opium gets involved. How this works is not simple. Feeling good depends on the state of the brain both physiologically and psychologically. To medicate our feeling of loneliness we alter our brains with drugs, including nicotine, caffeine and alcohol. However, we also search for the secure environment with others who support the same behavior (e.g., in neighborhood bars). Sometimes our environment is a solitary one, with the television our passive witness.

Our Cro-Magnon ancestors were probably as tall or taller than Americans, stronger, had more stamina, had little or no tooth decay, didn't smoke, drink alcohol and, when infectious diseases are taken into account, lived as long as we do. Today we search for the bonds of belonging which our ancestors apparently took for granted. We clearly cannot return to their way of life even if we wanted to. But we can do something creative about overcoming our self-constructed barriers which prevent our belonging and prolong our loneliness.

Questions

- Which substitute for belonging would you like to terminate?
- Do you need help? Where would you find the help you need?
- What will it take to get you to make the first step?
- What is holding you back from getting in touch with yourself and friends?

CHAPTER · SEVEN

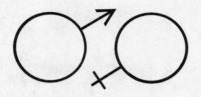

Making Friends With Yourself

---- * ----

*Be willing to acknowledge the hurt
of your own loneliness. We live in a lonely
time when no one is alone. Our mobile conditions
give most of us an enormous but shifting and,
therefore, superficial acquaintance. Let the
reality of your loneliness be a spur to
your own authentic quest.*

— Stuart Miller,
Men and Friendship

Solitude: Making An Attachment To Your Self

How can you be friends with someone, really intimate friends, if you can't be friends with yourself? Are you someone with whom you would like to be?

Ann's Story

Ann grew up without a father in an affluent university environment. Her alcoholic family was dominated by her grandmother and mother. Her younger brother began using cigarettes and marijuana during his early teen years. He graduated to cocaine and alcohol. By the time he was 25 he was in treatment. Ann admits to her own use of alcohol and drug addiction. But this good-looking brunette craves attachment. She explained, "I am learning to be alone with myself. I had to begin by just spending two or three minutes alone without doing something or planning what I was going to do. It was like withdrawal to be by myself. I would panic and call my therapist."

In her 34 years, Ann has had a series of husbands and lovers. Each has reinforced her addiction to hectic doing things, taking things in and sleeping around. Now, besides her therapy, she goes to several 12-Step programs a week. "I expect to increase my alone time by a few minutes each day," she says proudly.

Few people I have met are as frightened as Ann to be alone. However, many of us walk in the door after work or wake up to the companionship of the radio or television. We refuse to see our loneliness as an emotion telling us we need to belong. We need to feel real attachment: to others and *to ourselves*.

Creative Alone Time

I asked one Friendship Workshop to brainstorm as many creative things as they could to do alone. Many suggestions involved "doing things," such as gardening, cooking, reading, handicrafts and the like. Some people offered more time for reflection: peace, focusing, prayer, centering, thinking, dreaming, journal-keeping, yoga, massage, soaking in a hot tub and meditating.

Alone time, as all of our survey members know, is a time of rejuvenation. The child needs to retreat to the safe harbor. We need our quiet time to reflect on what has happened in our outer world. We need to sustain our inner world so we can cope with the outer. One person called it "spiritual refueling." We need to examine the mirrors of ourselves for any distortions. We need times free of stress and hassle to do this.

If we cannot be alone with ourselves, if we cannot separate from others, how can we be friends, that is, equal companions with others? We must be friends with ourselves first. Otherwise we become clinging, grabbing friendship leeches.

Anne Morrow Lindbergh put it this way:

> We are all, in the last analysis, alone. And this basic state of solitude is not something we have any choice about. . . . It is not the desert island, not the stony wilderness that cuts you from the people you love. It is the wilderness in the mind, the desert wastes in the heart through which one wanders lost and a stranger. When one is a stranger to oneself, then one is estranged from others too. If one is out of touch with oneself, then one cannot touch others.

So far we are flying on only one wing in our belonging: attachment to others. As we learned earlier, the companion to attachment is separation. Separation began at birth and developed into a sense of self-identity and self-esteem in that "Best of All Possible Worlds." We all know the difference between being alone and being lonely. Solitude is a time to be friends with oneself. It has similar expectations to friendships with others.

Requirements For Friendship With Yourself

Solitude is necessary to process our experience. It is a breathing in after a reaching out. Just as infants withdraw even in the presence of their mother, we need to withdraw to rejuvenate. Thoreau withdrew to Walden Pond, but remained in touch with Concord. I have spent several periods of my life living in solitude. Like Thoreau, "I went to the woods because I wished to live deliberately, to front only the essential facts of life, and see if I could not learn what it had to teach, and not when I came to die, discover that I had not lived. I did not wish to live what was not life, living is so dear, nor did I wish to practice resignation unless it was quite necessary."

As a 15 year old sequestered in a military school, I found I could sneak out early in the morning and hike through the farm country as the birds were waking up. The time alone beside a little stream and miniature falls filled an emptiness I could not name. Later I left a tenured position to live in the north Georgia mountains. There I practiced the basics of growing food, carrying water from the spring when the pump froze in the winter and relying on the wood I split for warmth.

Later still, I lived on a farm by a lake with a black Labrador retriever named Wendell (after the environmental poet Wendell Berry) as my only companion. Evenings on the lake were special times of quiet. One year egrets and cranes made the trees surrounding the lake their roost. They would come in flights of three or more. One circle around the lake was necessary to select the tree. The second time around, each bird would air-brake gently onto an unoccupied limb until the lake was sentineled by their shadows. Beavers would explore their own aquatic domain. The southern whippoorwill sang its sad meditation. Once in a while a screech owl interrupted the chorus of frogs.

During these periods I, like Thoreau, could find companionship when I wanted it. However, this farm retreat served as my escape from becoming too much of this world. I know it is a luxury to be able to ignore the pressures of modern fast-lane, addictive living. My escape was a luxury because it was more than most people can afford. However, if people don't make some escapes from their destructive attachments to the stresses of life, they will pay with fractured lives, broken relationships and high medical bills.

Your Own Expectations

We can look at the same expectations for friendships with others as qualities we expect in being friends with ourselves. *Commitment* to yourself requires sacrificing time with others to be alone. Remember that we only seem to have so much time and energy every day. Part of that time and energy must be devoted to nurturing ourselves.

Get out of the world for a while. Stop doing things. Turn off the radio and the television.

The world will get along without you. I learned that message, after week-long hiking trips in the Sierra Nevada Mountains or the Appalachians. The world was still there when I got back.

Don't grab the latest novel. Write in your journal. Write a personal letter telling your friend about the interior *you*. Or sit and watch nature change. Right now a black-hooded bird, the size of a sparrow, is exploring the limbs of a white pine 20 feet from my window. Over the past weeks a wasp has built her paper nest under my awning. She has been joined today by a second wasp. One of the cells is now capped. Nature is putting on a private show for my enjoyment alone.

Intimacy with self requires enough introspection, enough challenge to be frightening. We are capable of rejecting ourselves just as we reject others. We must risk this fear to get in touch with our soul.

Get to know your fantasies. Introduce yourself to your "Dark Side," as Jung called the part we would just as soon ignore. Tell yourself how much you appreciate you. What do you like about you? What don't you like? Write an autobiography. Who are you anyway?

Do you daydream? Don't be ashamed. *Fantasies are okay. You aren't required to act on them.* At times they express your Dark Side. At times your whimsical persona. Ask yourself what they are telling you just as you may question your night dreams.

Thoreau learned, "If one advances confidently in the direction of his dreams, and endeavors to live the life which he has imagined, he will meet with a success unexpected in common hours . . . If you have built castles in the air, your work need not be lost. That is where they should be. Now put the foundations under them."

Relaxation means you can just be alone without "doing something." You don't need the excuse of getting a tan to lie outside and watch the clouds scrub the sky blue or the thunderheads boil up into mountains.

We spend vacations and money to go someplace "to do something." We take pictures to show we've been there. Wait in lines. Ride the rides. See the sights. Hurry to the next pleasure. How about silently watching the wind polish the water? Watch the ocean change. Beachcomb without looking for anything in particular.

Courage is what it takes to confront oneself. The Speaker in Ecclesiastes says, "Here again, I saw emptiness under the sun: a lonely man without a friend, without son or brother, toiling endlessly yet never satisfied with his wealth — 'For whom,' he asks, 'am I toiling and denying myself the good things of life?' "

It takes courage to ask yourself what you are doing in this world. It takes courage to say to others, "I need time by myself."

The late confrontational environmentalist Edward Abbey also went to solitary places to confront life. In his *Desert Solitaire* he wrote, "Alone in the silence, I understand for a moment the dread which many feel in the presence of the primeval desert, the unconscious fear which compels them to tame, alter or destroy what they cannot understand, to reduce the wild and pre-human to human dimensions. Anything rather than confront directly the antihuman, the other world which frightens not through danger or hostility but in something far worse — its implacable indifference."

Engagement requires thinking about yourself. In remembering to take care of ourselves, we nurture our souls. Poet May Sarton called her *Journal of a Solitude*, "The intimate diary of a year in the life of a creative woman." She says, "It is only when we can believe that we are creating the soul that life has any meaning."

It may be that the emphasis on the "Me Generation" in the 1980s was a perversion of the need to learn to love oneself.

Unfortunately "Me" turned out to be the "public me" and not the private self: the soul.

Complicity has a sense of "Me" performing as several selves working together. We hear of people suffering from multiple personality disorders. We all have multiple personalities, our egos, super egos, Dark Sides, fantasy worlds. We wear many masks and we believe we are pretenders. No one knows the real me. Not even me. It is about time we became congruent.

Irene, a friend in my life for a brief time, explained her multiple personalities as different Greek goddesses. She even drew elegant pictures of these personalities. For this young, dark-haired woman, it was therapy. She could explain her behavior by identifying which goddess was speaking through her.

Acceptance is part of the vernacular of the '60s, "I'm okay." Today it is "Be yourself." Now that we know ourselves better, we can accept our idiosyncrasies as being part of our identity. If this person I am is not acceptable to me, how can I expect others to accept me?

Remember that unconditional love, the love we may have desired as children, is really acceptance. The image of a loving God accepting us wayward children is *agape.* Can we survive for long doing less than God? Can we accept our neighbor and not accept our Self?

Exercise

One full-length mirror and solitude required. Take off your clothes. Stand in front of the mirror. Look! Look at your hair. Why do you want to change it? What do you see in your eyes? Does your face look lopsided? Mouth too big, too small? Come on, be honest, you have been beating yourself up all these years about your appearance. Say it aloud to yourself. Look at your torso. Too skinny, too fat, too hairy? Breasts not the right size or shape? Legs too thin, penis too small, feet too big?

A chiropractor recently told me that most of his clients did not like themselves. "One woman, for instance, who was a real 10, complained her thighs were too big. Her thighs were great. You get a person naked and they tell you all the things they don't like about themselves. Everyone wants to be perfect."

We spend millions of dollars a year covering up and changing our exteriors without appraising our interiors. We buy different scents to cover up our natural body odors. We buy things to wear which shove our flesh and bones around. We do this to appear different than we are. In 1990 in the United States, 89,402 women had cosmetic surgery to enlarge their breasts and 42,888 more had breast reconstructions — most after mastectomies.

Oh sure, we attend workshops to change our interiors. We are physically touched at the barber and beauty shops. Gurus stroke our egos for money. Yet we avoid knowing and accepting who we are.

Take this opportunity to like yourself, naked, the way you arrived in this world without all those social pressures to look different than you are. Now say to that person in the mirror, "I accept you and all those imperfections which bothered you all these years." Say it until you have convinced yourself.

Getting Balance Back In Our Lives

Looking at solitude another way, we can say that *separation from others is becoming attached to yourself.* The important and paradoxical task is to find the balance between the different attachments. We can become so involved in seeking others that we ignore our souls. Or we can become so involved in navel-gazing that we ignore people attachments. Some famous, creative people have been isolates.

Anthony Storr examines the lives of Franz Kafka, Beatrix Potter, Rudyard Kipling, Alfred Lord Tennyson, Samuel Coleridge, Sylvia Plath, Michelangelo, John Keats, William Wordsworth, George Byron and Isaac Newton. Some of these had traumatic childhoods. His point is that they used their creations, which rose out of their solitude, to numb their depression and loneliness.

It is the existentialist's cry that there is no meaning. That frightens us. The lonely judge their lives as meaningless. We must learn to live the paradox of balancing attachment and separation. The paradox lived is the interaction of the public self in the mirror of friends and loved ones with the interior Self constructed from the perceptions of previous experience. Living the paradox is outgrowth and insight. The daily living of this paradox gives meaning to life.

Healing Our Anxieties

Sometimes these perceptions create false assumptions about ourselves and our relationships. Insight, looking within, can create distortions if our experience has been in dysfunctional families. Being alone with one's self can be destructive as well as creative. It is then that we need help to sort out and clean our knapsack.

What do you use to separate yourself from others? Watch television? Exercise? Read? Shop? Doing these things will not allow for insight. There are times when doing things is all we need. They are a change of speed and direction: relaxation. However, we must take time to challenge our lives.

You probably know Plato's dictum, "The life which is unexamined is not worth living." Plato had us viewing life as shadows on the wall of a cave. We may never enjoy the assurance of seeing our lives clearly. *Yet it is the process of living and not the goal that gives us meaning.* If we cannot go inside of ourselves alone, we can ask for help.

Getting Help With Our Insight

Friends are the first resource for those of us who need to clarify our expectations or to look in new directions. The Religious Society of Friends (Quakers) has developed a process known as "clearness" for those who want help in their sorting out. Friends meet together to help frame the questions rather than provide the answers. It sounds like a "Catch 22." We need friends to get clearness on being friends with others and with ourselves.

If you don't feel comfortable in asking friends, seek out a self-help group in the newspaper or from a national hot line number. Most of these are modeled on the 12-Step program. If you find others with similar values and a hopeful helpful attitude, stick with them. If not, keep searching. When you find one, be sure you aren't getting into another addiction.

You may want private counseling or therapy. There are so many different kinds that you may have to shop for a while. A sensitive counselor will not try to fit a client into a program which is not working for him or her. Remember that you are making a pretty firm attachment with this other person as part of your therapy. Your counselor may lead you to therapy groups.

I have helped form and maintain men's support groups for several years. In such groups, men learn to provide a safe place to hear about each other's interiors. They don't try to fix things, but to listen. A man confronting himself out loud frequently finds his own answers.

In exorcising the ghosts and coping with loneliness, we rely on several forms of belonging to help us belong to ourselves. Others may help us balance the spiral between attachment and separation. Only we can remove the load from our knapsack. Others may help us find the courage within ourselves to discard the burden which keeps us from ourselves and our friendships.

Questions

- Do you have times set aside to be with yourself?
- Do you daydream?
- What are the qualities which make *you* a good friend?
- Whom would you choose to call when you wanted to talk over a problem?
- Would you like to be considered by a friend as someone to call in an emergency?

CHAPTER EIGHT

Men Friends

❖

*And so it is. Life is so wonderful
and complex, and always relative. A man's
soul is a perpetual call and answer. He can never
be the call and the answer in one: between the dark
God and the incarnate man: between the dark soul
of woman, and the opposite dark soul of man:
and finally, between the souls of man and
man, strangers to one another, but answers.
So it is forever, the eternal weaving of calls and
answers, and the fabric of life woven and perishing
again. But the calls never cease, and the answers
never fail for long. And when the fabric
becomes grey and machine-made, some
strange clarion-call makes men
start to smash it up.
So it is.*

— D.H. Lawrence, *Kangaroo*

Our models of friendship between men are fractured. We see male buddies in war, in sports, in the bar, but something is missing in men's lives. It is helpful for both men and women to look at the old models to see what was expected in the past and what may be possible now. Men can identify what is missing. Women can see what may be different from their experience.

One Tribal Experience

As darkness descends on the Kalahari Desert, the bonfire sends sparks rocketing toward the moon. The women, gathered in a group on one side, start a rhythmic clapping and chanting. The men begin a shuffling dance around the fire. After hours of a short-stepping march, single-file, the men wear a deep trench in the ground. With a few short breaks, they continue tramping into the first purple of dawn.

Suddenly a dancer pitches back, eyes rolling, shaking in a kind of cataleptic state. The other men run to him, holding, patting and rubbing his limbs and body. He has become a healer. In an altered state of consciousness, he is cared for by his fellow dancers. He may rise and touch the women and children to take any sickness or evil from them.

The dance begins again. Another man breaks the circle and rushes around the camp. A fellow dancer follows to care for him, to make sure he doesn't run into something or burn himself. He is led back to the group and continues circling with glazed eyes.

As the dance continues, the sun blasts over the hills. The men begin to collapse in a heap, limbs and heads on top of one another. Then they slowly rise and search for shade to sleep off their fatigue. The !Kung San's healing Trance Dance has ended.

Social anthropologist Marjorie Shostak considers the !Kung San society a pattern for most human societies before agriculture. These hunter-gatherers are "the most successful adaptation people have yet made to their environment," she concludes. Several of the visitors who have lived with these people for any length of time agree they are "the most talkative people in the world." The men sit close, touching one another, talking about hunting, retelling stories. They have been the subject of sweet, tense and commercially successful films like *The Gods Must Be Crazy*.

!Kung Friends

"The !Kung are a fiercely egalitarian people and have low tolerance for arrogance, stinginess, and aloofness," Richard Lee reports. They use ridicule as a leveling device. Shostak believes they demonstrate the nearest to equality between the sexes of any culture, although there is a division of labor. Men still dominate as spokespersons, but a water-hole area can "belong" to either sex and clans are matrilineal. The married man moves in with his wife's family (like the Hopi in the Southwestern United States).

Another anthropologist observed, "Friendly bonding behavior predominates in the interaction of adults, and these people spend many hours a day grooming each other, chatting, sharing a pipe, and playing with their children."

They establish friendship bonds through an elaborate ritual. *Hxaro* begins with a gift. The recipient, if one of a couple, confers with the partner to determine whether they wish to include this person in their complex friendship bonds. The exchange of gifts goes on for at least a year before the friendship is considered firm. Then that person resides "in the heart" of the other, each friend with responsibility for the other. There is nearly equal sex distribution, male-male, male-female, sharing *hxaro*. Most of the time spent not getting food (more than half the week) is spent maintaining social relationships, gossiping, while making gifts.

Similar to *hxaro* bonding in the same people, George Silberbauer emphasizes "joking partners," keeping each other in line by castigation. It is like the friendly banter seen in our neighborhood tavern. The men and women have an elaborate system of sexual jokes: the bow "is a bawdy metaphor for the penis." A man saying, "I have no bow," means "he is at a loss sexually." Insult is frequently over sexual ability. When conflict arises, a feast may be declared to remove the stress by using an etiquette of friendliness. Most decisions are reached by consensus — talking out a common pool of information.

Cross-Sex Association

In the !Kung band, children play together building their own "village" and playing house much like Western children, practicing adult skills. As the boys get older, they play hunting, make bows and practice sex with the girls. Shostak says there is no word for virginity in !Kung language. Girls are married as early as 14. The husband must respect her possible lack of interest in sex at that early age.

Nisa, the subject of Shostak's biography, had two husbands before menstruation because she was not pleased with the first. Nisa emphasized, "If a girl grows up without learning to enjoy sex, her mind doesn't develop normally." Promiscuity spices the adult life. However, because they live so intimately, promiscuity is hard to cover up and creates the major conflicts in the band.

The Turnbulls describe similar growing up among the "forest people," the Mbuti. They play together until puberty. The girls have a special puberty rite. Boys are expected to be responsible not to get a girl pregnant. A child calls every man and woman in the band "Father" and "Mother."

Grooming and relaxing for the Mbuti men means painting one another and picking each other for lice. These pygmies bond with the villagers on the edge of the forest. They hold joint initiation ceremonies. For boys between nine and eleven years of age, initiation lasts three months and involves circumcision. The initiation represents the death of the boy as a child and his rebirth as a man, bringing him "under control of the ancestral tribal spirits."

Men In Literature:
From Gilgamesh To The Odd Couple

Men have a history of bonding by *doing*. They meet adversity together and initiate their male children by ordeal. Whether in the band society still in evidence today or as recorded in written history and literature, men make friendships through physical intimacy.

It is only in North American culture that men have become alienated and wary of one another. In other cultures and in other times, men have enjoyed a rich tradition of friendship.

This tradition of friendship is recorded in the earliest known writings at the dawn of civilization. We discover, in what is now known as Iraq, one of the oldest written narratives of male friendship. This is the Epic of Gilgamesh, who was king of the Sumerian city of Urak. To tame this wild king, the goddess Aruru creates a wild man of the steppe, Enkidu. After taming Enkidu with a woman (an archetypical theme), Aruru brings him to Urak.

There, Gilgamesh and Enkidu perform an earth-shattering wrestling match before becoming fast friends. They undergo epic exploits together, as Herakles (Hercules) and other Greek heroes will several thousand years later. Enkidu dies and Gilgamesh, mad with grief, first becomes wild, taking on the persona of his soul brother. In a timeless quest, Gilgamesh then searches for immortality before reconciling to his own mortality.

Classic Friends

We still read of the legendary male friendships glorified during the classical Greek and Roman periods:

Achilles and Patroclus. When Achilles refuses to fight, intending to annoy Agamemnon, Patroclus puts on Achilles' armor and is killed by Hector. Enraged, Achilles in turn kills Hector and routs the Trojans.

Castor and Pollux. According to Greek mythology, these twin sons of Zeus and Leda adventure together with Jason in quest of the Golden Fleece (a Holy Grail legend). Eventually they become the constellation Gemini. Another male pair in the Argonaut epic are Herakles and Hylas, his squire and friend, who is lost to Herakles through drowning.

David and Jonathan. Upon Jonathan's death in battle with the Philistines, David laments "Your love for me was wonderful, surpassing the love of women." (II Sam i, 26.)

Damon and Pythias. Damon takes his friend Phintias' place to be executed to enable Phintias to return home and say farewell. When Phintias returns for his execution, both are freed.

Another Greek hero, Pirithous, tests Theseus before the two men become compatriots in stealing women — Helen of Troy, when she was a child, and Persephone in Hades. When they get caught by Pluto, Hercules sets out to rescue Theseus. Pirithous is still sitting in hell for all we know.

Another wrestling match occurs between Dionysus (Bacchus) and his lover Ampelos. Later, when Ampelos dies, he turns into the infamous grapevine.

Aristotle says in *Ethics*, "That friendships of this quality should be rare is only what is expected, for men of that quality [of goodness] are rare. And besides goodness they need time and intimacy to establish perfect friendship. As the proverb has it, you cannot learn to know a man until you have eaten a peck of salt with him. Wishing to be friends is quick work, but friendship is a slow-ripening fruit."

The Arthurian legend, which can be traced in English literature to the seventh century, is about a Briton leader who fights against the Saxons in the fifth century. The story of a fellowship, magic, betrayal and a search for the Holy Grail keeps cropping up from the twelfth century to contemporary literature.

In France, the legend of good King Charlemagne and his 12 paladins recapitulates the Arthurian myth. Two of the bodyguards, Roland and Oliver, fight one another for five days at the end of which there is no victor. The battle cements their friendship. They die together guarding the rear of Charlemagne's army.

Equally moving, the twelfth-century French romance of Amis and Amiles ends as Amiles kills his children in the belief that their sacrifice will cure his friend's leprosy.

The father/son conflict pervades Shakespeare's plays. They are also crowded with male friendships: the ribald camaraderie of Prince Hal and Falstaff, the teenage bravado in *Romeo and Juliet*, the friends as enemies in *Coriolanus* and *The Winter's Tale* and the betrayed in *Henry V* and *Two Gentlemen of Verona*.

Polonius advises Laertes in *Hamlet*, "The friends thou hast and their adoption tried, Grapple them to thy soul with hoops of steel." [I.3] Hamlet, in explaining his friendship with Horatio, concludes, "Give me that man that is not passion's slave, and I will wear him in my heart's core, aye, in my heart of hearts as I do thee." [III.2] And Hamlet is betrayed by two false friends.

More Contemporary Friends

Poet Walt Whitman proposed that the love of comrades would make America "the most splendid race the sun ever shone upon." He warns, "I say democracy infers such loving comradeship, as its most inevitable twin or counterpart, without which it will be incomplete, in vain and incapable of perpetuating itself."

What has happened to destroy Whitman's dream of American comradeship? Greed, competition, homophobia, missing fathers, social disapproval, jealousy? A combination of these conditions? Our contemporary writers have not given up either in the novel, the theater or the movies. James Leo Herlihy's *Midnight Cowboy* was twisted into a film flawed by homosexual innuendo not present in the novel.

It is clear that Brick and Skipper were not homosexuals in *Cat on a Hot Tin Roof*, but that fear is the focus of the play. The film version with Elizabeth Taylor and Paul Newman, produced in a more puritanical atmosphere than today, leaves out important dialogue explaining the love between the football players. The more recent television version with Jessica Lange and Tommy Lee Jones does not flinch from this.

Nikos Kanzantazakis, writing *Zorba the Greek* while starving during the German occupation of Greece, explored the struggle of man with the God within himself and around him, the images of manhood and womanhood, and the love men can have for one another.

The friendship epic *Lonesome Dove* by Larry McMurtry was also turned into a television film. It epitomizes the grand sweep of bonding between men of the American West. The commitment the men have for one another overshadows other buddy films such as *Butch Cassidy and the Sundance Kid, Easy Rider* and *That Championship Season.*

One of the greatest literary friendships occurs between Sherlock Holmes and Dr. Watson in the Arthur Conan Doyle stories. Dr. Watson's role is central as the narrator, equal and friend; not the "talkative, bumbling, never close to understanding the situation at hand" character as critic Leonard Malkin calls the Nigel Bruce-Basil Rathbone film relationship.

The friendship began with Holmes and Watson deciding to share rooms. Holmes says on their first meeting, "Let me see — what are my other shortcomings? I get in the dumps at times and don't open my mouth for days on end. You must not think I am sulky when I do that. Just let me alone and I'll soon be all right. What have you to confess now? It's just as well for two fellows to know the worst of each other before they begin to live together."

Neil Simon put two men together in *The Odd Couple*, a comedy with depth. When Felix, played on stage by Art Carney, is kicked out by his wife, he comes to the men's Friday night poker game. Oscar, whose portrayal rocketed Walter Matthau to fame after several years of villain roles, fusses over Felix and attempts to get him drunk. First massaging Felix's back, Oscar scolds Felix for not relaxing.

Felix replies, "I thought you were my friend."

Oscar: "That's why I can talk to you like this. Because I love you almost as much as you do."

When Felix moves in, the play becomes a parody of marriage, Felix the perfect wife, Oscar the perfect slob. Finally, Oscar kicks Felix out with, "We're getting an annulment!"

Felix disappears and the entire poker crew is worried. Murray, a married policeman, sums it up: "We all know he's impossible, but he's still our friend, and he's out on the street, and I'm still worried about him."

When Felix arrives, it is obvious that both he and Oscar have changed — grown up.

D.H. Lawrence And Brotherhood

Another modern advocate of a brotherhood of men was D.H. Lawrence. His *Women in Love* would have been better called "Men in Love." Two men spar over friendship, never quite making the connection. At their final parting, Gerald complains about the hurt and attraction he suffers with Gudrun. Birkin replies bitterly, "I've loved you as well as Gudrun, don't forget." Gerald answers skeptically, "Have you? Or do you think you have?"

Following Gudrun's ultimate rejection and Gerald's violent response, Gerald wanders off to die in the cold. Learning of Gerald's death, Birkin breaks down. He believes that if Gerald had loved him, it would have made a difference — he would still be alive. Birkin tells his wife Ursula that he believed in another kind of love between men. In the film version of the novel, the last frame freezes on Ursula's incredulous face.

The theme of men's love recurs in Lawrence's *Kangaroo* and *The Plumed Serpent*. In the ensuing years no one, to my knowledge, has taken up Lawrence's passion for a mystical marriage between two men. I am sure homophobia has kept men from viewing *Women in Love* as a demand for loving relationships between men and from describing those dreams realistically.

Lawrence and his biographers are ambiguous about his attitude toward homosexuality. Difficulties in finding a publisher caused a nearly six-year delay in publication of *Women In Love*. A critic writing in *John Bull*, September 1921, saw the homosexual implications and demanded that the police seize the book as they had *The Rainbow* several years before.

Anais Nin understood Lawrence's message. She wrote, "There was an unknown world within the known. He had a vision. Will it take us one hundred years to understand Lawrence's vision as it took us one hundred years to understand Blake's?"

I believe Lawrence anticipated the profound disturbance that women's liberation would make. He plumbed the depths of his psyche to discover how men might react. He gave us much to consider, sometimes adolescent in perspective, mostly idealistic, frequently narcissistic, often pessimistic. It is not only a shame but blatant homophobia to ignore his message by labeling either Lawrence or his vision as homosexual.

It may be that Lawrence's closest friend and model for Gerald, John Middleton Murry, should have the last word on Lawrence's homophilic ideal. Murry and his wife Katherine Mansfield, a model for Gudrun, lived with Lawrence and his wife Frieda for two months as *Women in Love* was being written.

Murry, the object of Lawrence's desire for a close and lasting friendship, wrote in the *London Times Literary Supplement*, March 13, 1930, following Lawrence's death: "Friendship was to him a blood-brotherhood, an absolute and inviolable loyalty, not to a person, but to the impersonal godhead beneath. I do not believe that he ever found the friendship after which he hungered; and perhaps this was the tragedy of his life. The men he knew were incapable of giving that which he demanded. It was not their fault, though in his heart of hearts he believed it was."

However, if you conclude that Lawrence was the only author with this vision of male bonding, listen to Jack London's dream of living with a "great Man-Comrade" in a letter to his future wife, Charmian.

> It was plain that . . . I could never hope to find that comradeship, that closeness, that sympathy and understanding whereby the man and I might merge and become one for love and life. How can I say what I mean? This man should be so much one with me that we could never misunderstand . . . He should be delicate and tender, brave and game; sensitive as he pleased in the soul of him and in the body of him unfearing and unwitting of pain . . . Do you see, my dear one, the man I am trying to picture for you?

What does this smorgasbord of literature have in common? It certainly isn't comprehensive, but it is indicative of the variety of ways men love other men. While most of these examples describe this love, shared intimacy is much less frequent. Intimacy is experienced in active association and support rather than the verbal sharing women expect with women's friendships. Once the reader has been sensitized to the subtleties of friendship, a world of other examples opens up.

Men In Groups

As dangerous as male groups may be, the paradox remains, according to Lionel Tiger, that men need masculine association. He observes:

> Males bond in terms of either a pre-existent object of aggression or a concocted one . . . men in continuous association aggress

against the environment in much the same way as men and women
in continuous association have sexual relations.

Fraternal Organizations And Secret Societies

As I have said, rites of passage assisted by our elders have all
but disappeared. We recognize that men and women do need
support groups. It is the inappropriate behavior of some of these
groups that we fear. The traditional forms of male bonding have
suffered a diminished membership over the past several decades.

Since the mid-1800s at least 2,000 fraternal organizations have
appeared in North America, most exclusively male. About 450
still exist. Some were benefit societies providing insurance for
their members, while others were secret orders providing fraternal fellowship. Freemasonry has lost 25 percent of its 1950s
membership while the Odd Fellows and Knights of Pythias show
greater decreases.

Reasons for the formation of a new fraternal organization are
varied and frequently secret. Political organizations from the local
ward to the national caucus rooms have contributed as much to
male camaraderie as to social maintenance. This formerly exclusive male club is no longer a haven for men's high jinks. When
political change or maintenance of the status quo and economic
security are discounted, the remaining male organizations cite
"fun loving" as motive for formation.

Originally called Corks, the Elks (BPOE) started as merry-
making singers and actors in a New York alehouse. The Ku Klux
Klan was "founded by Judge Thomas M. Jones in 1865 or 1866 in
Pulaski, Tennessee . . . eager for some fun and amusement."

However, fun is usually not enough to sustain interest over a
long period of time. Soon ritual, pageantry and secrecy are added
to create feelings of acceptance and to promote exclusivity and
continuity. A former Klansman observed that a majority of people
who join the Ku Klux Klan are poor whites who feel hopelessly
rejected by society and shut out of the mainstream. By joining
the Klan, they hope to find acceptance. Their bonding with a
group of their peers is focused on the issue of laying blame on
another group of "outsiders" for their troubles.

Male secret societies have existed throughout the ages and have been a force for both good and evil. But people on the outside of the inner circle have often been suspicious of the concealed plans, agreements and contracts of the clandestine group. Such groups have been outlawed or repressed in the past and forced underground. Current efforts to end male exclusivity may not be solely an expression of feminist egalitarianism, but also reflect a more profound psychological awareness that aggression might be reduced all around by letting in other influences.

Tiger points out that bonding reduces aggression *within* a group, but increases aggression toward outsiders. He views secret societies as inherently aggressive since they invite hostility and fear among the nonmembers, paradoxically, either because the group is part of the political power structure or an anti-government faction.

Loose Associations

What has replaced the fraternal organization? Although luncheon clubs, such as the Rotary, Kiwanis and Lions continue with their noon relaxation, business connections and benevolence, they hardly create the closeness of the secret society. Three models still exist: groups such as the Bohemian Club of San Francisco (founded much like the Elks), the fabled Southern Good Ole Boy network and the neighborhood tavern.

High Rollers At Summer Camp

The Bohemian Club has sponsored a two-week retreat for the elite at Bohemian Grove, California, every summer for more than a hundred years. Memberships and guest lists read like the "Who's Who" of the corporate/political world: George Schultz, Henry Kissinger, Gerald Ford, Alexander Haig and Ronald Reagan, to drop a few names. Although the guests go to great lengths to "cremate care" (an elaborate ceremony initiating the retreat), there is little doubt that carefree conviviality creates a camaraderie which extends past the borders of the grove to the reins of power.

It is the common theme of the businessman that he is only a word away from work when he plays, drinks and eats. Every action must be to some purpose. Even the "cremation of care" at the Bohemian Grove must be carefully orchestrated.

GOBs

The Southern Good Ole Boy belongs to an organization as
loose as the Bohemian Club is tight. According to two Southern
ladies, Rosemary Daniell and Florence King, the Good Ole Boy is
bonded to his brothers out of the fear that he is a loser. He still
hasn't got over the Civil War. And he fears he is impotent socially,
if not physically.

Daniell observes, "Any woman who wants to see the term *male
bonding* made concrete need only complain of one good ole boy to
another, and watch the glaze form instantaneously over the eye-
balls of her listener. It is a lens through which it is impossible to
see any flaw in one's brother. 'He's jes' a good ole boy!' is a phrase
a Southern man will use to excuse anything from armed robbery
to bigamy."

King reports that the good ole boys "hang out on porches and
benches in an unconscious military formation." Bonding between
these losers (Daniell finds that they are not limited to the South)
and between the affluent Bohemians arises out of much the same
fear. Security is dependent on their ability to exert apparent control over and manipulate their environments. Both present images
of the worst kind of patriarchy so derided by feminists. The
increase in KKK membership throughout the United States probably has its basis in the same fear of impotence in work, community and sex.

Drinking Buddies

The tavern is the center of social life for the blue-collar male.
E.E. Le Masters described the interactions occurring in a laboring
class, family tavern of the early Seventies in *Blue-Collar Aristocrats*.
He found that the men were secure in their occupations and peer
group support. Stress occurred in marriage if the wife brought
home from her job middle-class expectations of status and of
companionship. The men enjoyed ". . . male companionship (such
as) to drink beer, shoot pool, play cards, pitch horseshoes, bowl,
fish, hunt and talk . . ."

The men didn't have the juke box on unless women were present because they enjoyed ". . . the music of their own conversation." How far their camaraderie went in supporting each other

Le Masters leaves ambiguous. The banter around the bar may have diffused some personal crises. I find it quite revealing of these men's gender identity that, while they are violently anti-homosexual and must leave or fight if called a "queer," they would dance together when a woman wasn't available.

Men will always find ways of drinking together. Frank DeFord, when senior writer for *Sports Illustrated*, called the nation's sports stadiums "the largest saloons" in the United States. As a bartender at a local pub, I watched this chumminess lubricated with alcohol. The same stories, the same men, the same jokes day after day were mostly what these aging men lived for.

Filling The Need

Men are creating new forms of association as the more traditional ones fail to meet their needs. The middle-class bar, the football party, the soccer, rugby, baseball, bowling and even running teams allow gender exclusivity under the guise of a "new" interest in physical fitness.

Psychotherapists Anne Steinman and Dean David Fox of the City University of New York regret that men are losing opportunities to meet with other men in social interactions and ". . . argue against the notion that all social institutions and all social practices must or should be integrated [by sex] in the adult world or in the new world we would want to create for the children to come."

Harold Lyon, a former West Point trained ranger and contributor to our nomenclature of friendship, speaks from personal experience when he says, "Men face a special kind of loneliness in life: the loneliness of the hunter . . . [which is eased when] men tend to seek one another out, to give one another the kind of understanding and empathy which either women cannot give or which men have not learned to accept from women." This thought was echoed one evening in a men's support group. "Men have a loneliness women cannot assuage," mused one man.

So men invent methods to associate: sports, sports viewing, strip shows, "smokers" and so on. Carol, a 30-year-old stripper at a neighborhood bar, observed that a "lady psychologist's" report of her dancing missed the point: ". . . She neglected to mention the fact that one of the main reasons men come here is the camaraderie among themselves. I'm not talking about homosexuality. I'm talking about being able to touch, pat each other on the back, hug."

A Men's Movement Of Sorts

The picture of men estranged from one another may already be changing. Out in the woods men are gathering to beat drums, to dance freely, to tell their stories, to recite their poetry and to open their wounds and share their pain. Television reporter Bill Moyers gave impetus to this phenomenon with his interview of Robert Bly. Not wishing to be another movement guru, Bly still symbolizes the uncovering of men's pain. Bly, with his disciples, can bring together several hundred men for a day of drumming, storytelling and poetry. These gatherings give men an opportunity to rage, cry and support other men in their self-discovery.

Such a gathering of men hearkens back to the Victorian men's club such as The Red Men, who emulated Native Americans without including them. During every era when masculinity has been questioned, men have responded with secret societies, sports and initiations for boys such as the Boy Scouts. In our present society the military is the only legitimate initiation and acceptance ritual into the community of men. For some, prisons serve the same role.

Why Men Love War

War and sports are vehicles for male bonding. Gwynne Dyer in his book *War* observes:

> What really enables men to fight is their own self-respect and a special kind of love that has nothing to do with sex or idealism. Very few men have died in battle when the movement actually arrived, for the United States of America or for the sacred cause of Communism or even for their homes and families. If they had any choice in the matter at all, they choose to die for each other and for their own vision of themselves . . . And you'll find that people who pursue the aphrodisiac of combat or whatever you want to call it are there because they're friends; the same people show up in the same wars time and again.

Neil Simon ends his autobiographical film *Biloxi Blues* by reflecting that his years in the army were the best time of his life. Not because of the army or the men, but because they experienced the time when they were young together. The passage of years added affection for his buddies.

Philip Caputo echoes this feeling in *A Rumor Of War:*

> I have also attempted to describe the intimacy of life in infantry battalions, where the communion between men is as profound as any between lovers. Actually it is more so. It does not demand for its sustenance the reciprocity, the pledges of affection, the endless reassurances required by the love of men and women. It is, unlike marriage, a bond that cannot be broken by a word, by boredom or divorce or by anything other than death. . . . Such devotion, simple and selfless, the sentiment of belonging to each other, was the one decent thing we found.

Dyer goes on to say, "The basic combat unit, a small group of men bound together by strong male ties of loyalty and trust, was a time-tested system that worked, and [the generals] were reluctant to tamper with it by adding an additional, unknown factor [women] to the equation."

War and sports may be the modern equivalents of primitive hunting parties. Returning to his memories of fighting in Vietnam, author William Broyles lists several reasons why men love war. First it is the comradeship, the brotherly love. He says, "War is the only utopian experience most of us ever have. . . . No one is allowed to be alone."

Also, war is a game, a great thrill. It is initiation into the power of life and death. It has raw beauty and it heightens all appetites — sex included. It is an opportunity for attachment and can become addictive.

Questions

- Should men have exclusive all-male groups? Why?
- Would you belong to a same-sex group?
- What would you get out of it if you did belong?
- Can women become "one of the boys"? Why would they want to?

Two Men From Different Cultures

India

My interest in men and friendship was sparked by a young man reporting his experience in India. He found men close, supportive, even holding hands, with no homosexual expectations. He wanted the same encounter when he returned to the United States.

I decided to interview a native of India who practices pathology at a major American hospital. Dr. Bhagirath Majmudar grew up in an India which began to change shortly after World War II, when India won its independence from Great Britain. He recalls his schooling: "Men are for men in India. I come from a very disciplinarian society. In my lower schooling 95 percent were boys — all through high school. In my undergraduate years 75 percent were men. The women came from rich, cultured homes and they were expected to be very smart.

"No, I don't think men are more intelligent than women. But I have seen the best only. When I went to medical school, 55 percent were men, and now it has changed to 45 percent. Women doctors are not looked down on as they are in the United States.

"Men in India grow up to prefer the company of men. We learn to share intimate thoughts. We didn't spend much time with women. If a woman is our age we call her 'sister.' Yes, women were treated as subordinate, but with much respect. It is a paradox that we have very erotic art and yet are very respectful of women. In the United States, women are treated as objects. In school I would address my class, 'brothers and sisters.' In college — 'ladies and gentlemen.' We called older women 'Mother.'

"Boys in India are very close; we have no fear of sex. Whereas boys in this country have shallow superficial relationships, in India we have deep meaningful dialogue with each other. Always testing, always trying to find out meaning — struggling to find our identity. We argue about everything. At about 22, a man begins to start thinking clearly.

"In this country if you spend a lot of weekends talking with friends you have invited over — well, you're not allowed. In India men get together all the time. We argue and shout and when it's over, we are still friends. Women in India do the same thing.

Women are welcome in our hot arguments. Sometimes they listen, sometimes they argue too. Our talk is like the Greeks, loud and noisy.

"The main disadvantage when I was growing up was that I learned nothing about women. Yes, it is the same way in the United States. Until the last ten years men did not need to understand women. Women had to understand men. My wife and I, we have learned together. She was the first woman I got to know in depth. We stumbled into how to get along."

Dr. Majmudar visited his homeland recently and confided, "I had to find my childhood and college friends to renew our old acquaintances." In response to a question about competition, he replied, "No, we are pleased when a friend achieves more . . . he is to be honored. We don't compete like you do here."

Dr. Majmudar's remembrances of his growing up male are confirmed by an Indian woman in one of my workshops. She was quite upset that she could find few men here willing to date without wanting sex. She said, "In India I could call up any one of many men friends to go out with to a show with no fear of other expectations."

Iran

I also had the opportunity to interview Dr. M. Hosein Abgahari, a native of Iran, who has lived in the United States for ten years. I talked with him about his friendships in an Atlanta area college, where he teaches economics. Married before leaving Iran, the Abgaharis have two children and a relationship that represents a transition from traditional Iranian male-female roles to a more modern attitude — set back by the revolution.

"Soon after I arrived in the United States, I invited one of my friends to join me," said Dr. Abgahari. "He came to live with us in our apartment six months later for one year since he didn't have enough money to live on his own. Then he went to school in another city. Since he is unmarried, he has the freedom to join us all the time — summer, December. We traveled as a family seeing this country.

"Then I started meeting other Iranians. Usually you are not going to have a lot of friends. Those who say they are friends of

everyone are not friends of anyone because they cannot understand the principle. Ten friends is the most.

"The concept of friendship in Iran is completely different from
the concept I see here. By Iranian definition I cannot say that I
have any American friends.

"In Iran you meet different people, start going out with people
in your neighborhood, in high school. [The grade schools and
high schools were sexually segregated when he went to school,
were integrated in 1976, then segregated once more with the
revolution.] You start talking. When you establish friendship, it is
a strong commitment. I cannot use the word 'love,' no. But the
relationship is very strong. We use the concept of love only for
relationships between boys and girls. We never use the concept
of love for other things like here — I 'love' my pet, this furniture
or what. Not at all.

"Friendship means that I am totally behind my friend for any
kind of support he may need, financial or whatever. In our view
of friendship, nothing is secret: Your friend knows everything
about you, financial, whom you are dating, whatever. There's no
limitation. If my friend has a financial problem, he doesn't ask for
money. If I have money it is my responsibility to help. You never
ask for interest. Any time he has enough money, he is going to
pay you back. You don't ask for it.

"In any society there are many people who may want to exploit
you, misuse the relationship. You have to develop a mutual trust.
Of course, after some months, a year, you can see if the relationship is going to be a friendship. If you see something you don't
like, be careful. But with friendship, any time, day or night, that
you need anything, you are sure your friend is behind you. You
have somebody to whom you can say, 'Okay, I have this problem.'

"Your friend has more information about you than even your
brothers or sisters or parents. There may be some things we hide
from them, but we never hide anything from our friends."

Abgahari described a friend who had a gambling problem. Abgahari continued to help him, even when his friend broke a promise not to gamble. Abhahari lent his friend $2,000 dollars to pay
back gambling debts.

Abgahari gave another example: "I have a friend here in the
United States who was going to school when the revolution hap-

pened. His family couldn't send him money. He was married and
had kids. It was a problem and a problem for me. I said, 'Okay,
you finish school, you get a job.' And he and his entire family
came and lived with us.

"If I am going out of town, I call my friend and tell him that my
wife and children will be alone, watch them. He comes here, he
takes them to his house. If I say, 'You should come and stay here,'
they come.

"You can argue with your friend. You have different political
stands. Since you are going to have a lot of discussion, after some
time your lines become closer and closer. We try to be rational.
Okay, if you are arguing rationally, if you convince me, that is it.
I accept your views."

When asked how he keeps up his friendships, Abgahari replies,
"My telephone bill all the time is over $100. At least once a week
we are calling them, they are calling us. [He has friends in Texas
and Pennsylvania as well as Atlanta.] The first occasion we have,
we go visit a friend.

"The main obstacle to friendships in America is material. If I
am going to spend this much time with a friend, I am not going
to make this much money. Everything is measured materially. In
our friendship we don't think about the material. What is important is that relationship. Materialism has become part of the American culture."

I asked about the perception of two men together as homosexual: "There is no such suspicion. We kiss each other. If we are
walking in the street, it is hand in hand. You call your friend
every day if you live in the same city. We have this difficulty in
America. When I go to the airport, we usually kiss each other. We
are under pressure. Okay? Should we? Forget it! We kiss, let
them think what they want, but they are wrong. [He describes a
hierarchy of touch where one shakes hands with acquaintances
and kisses friends.] Sometimes you may disappoint someone. You
may kiss one person in a line and shake hands with another."

I asked if he could have friendships with women without sex.
"Most of the time sexual relationship is expected. You can develop
friendship without sex. But the majority think if you have established friendship, you are going to have sex.

"I had seven years of close friendship with my wife [before marriage] without sex. When I announced that I wanted to get married, she was surprised. 'How do you want to marry me? I cannot imagine that we can establish and develop an intimate relationship.'

"I became her brother's friend first. I started to know her brothers, mother, father. I was always going to their house. I was invited to her birthday party. There were six girls in the group also. We developed a relationship in college. I was friends with my wife all through college and work. When I decided to come here, I invited her to lunch and told her that I wanted to get married. She couldn't believe it. She said, 'I know you well, let me think about this.'

"All of our friends were surprised. They said there is nothing between you. But I know her, her ideas. She knows me; there's no conflict. We couldn't have got married if we hadn't been friends. Both families were trying to create some problems, but they couldn't do anything because we were friends. If we didn't know each other very well, we would have given up. I have committed myself to this friend. I am not going to give up at any price.

"Traditionally there is much information that your friend has that your wife doesn't. But in my case I am open with my wife. In the younger generation we try to share. I still am friends with my wife [who is receiving her Ph.D. in microbiology]."

We could go on discovering friendships among other first generation Americans from, for example, Greece, Italy and the Middle East, but the conclusion would be the same. It is easier to find intimate friendships among men of older, more stable cultures. There is no doubt in my mind that men hunger for the intimacy of men just as intensely as they do for the intimacy of women. They use different forms of physical intimacy to get close — to get in touch with the other person. One form is the sweaty proximity of adversity; the other form, for some, is sex.

Questions

- What have you learned?
- What more would you like to know about these subjects?

- Have you changed or deepened your expectations for friendship?
- Before going on to the next chapter about women's friendships, how would you compare men's and women's same-sex friendships?
- How many times in reading this chapter did the word "love" shock you? Did you think of sex?

CHAPTER NINE

Women's Friendships

———※———

*Indeed a woman without a
best friend is a very lonely woman . . .
Women unguardedly confide in each other with
an ease that often astounds men. Sharing is
not a concession, a particularly difficult
struggle, an extraction; rather it is part and
parcel of women's relating. It is second
nature, a habit, a way of being. Not
sharing feels odd. A holding back that
feels almost like a betrayal.*

— Luise Eichenbaum and Susie Orbach,
Between Women

Comedian Carol Burnett and actress Julie Andrews are best friends. Through the years following their meeting in 1961, through husbands, divorce and children, they have kept in touch. The something that clicked at their first meeting, they learned many years later, was their common bond of surviving alcoholic families. Burnett explains, "We're both caretakers."

Their camaraderie arises from a sharing of their talents, their shows and their lives. Progressing from being "chums" to being sisters, Burnett senses "a deep, deep bond, almost a spiritual tie." This is a connection both D.H. Lawrence and Jack London only dreamed of.

If men's friendships are based on physical intimacy usually associated with adversity, women's friendships are quite different. They are based on verbal intimacy, shared secrets. But shared adversity is also present in their lives. Their physical intimacy is the knowledge of their common natural experiences — menstruation, childbirth, menopause — and emotional ones, such as identification with and separation from Mother.

As a male who has spent many years observing the behavior of other men forming — and blocked from — friendships, I tend to consider men's friendships more problematic and view women's friendships as easier and more natural to their gender. However, many women — some in my own workshops — disagree with me. Let us agree that the comparison is relative, and perhaps, in the final analysis, can only be subjective.

History

The image of paleolithic women in a band society is one of responsibility: gathering, preparing and cooking most of the food. Women handled most of the infant and child care. Among the !Kung San, it was the women who decided when to move the band and which marriage partners to accept into the band for their daughters. Clan history was matrilineal. Women held property rights to clan water holes.

Among the Iroquois, the women alone could declare war. However, to believe that at one time a human matriarchy existed is to believe a myth, according to historian Gerda Lerner.

As more and more property was acquired by individual families, men began to dominate the family, the tribe and one another. Property needed to be defended, then territory. Next, women themselves were considered property because they produced laborers and were themselves laborers. Throughout this history of subjugation, women retained their own culture of "the sisterhood."

Lerner concludes:

> In the past, and now, many emergent women [she also calls them thinking women] have turned to other women as love objects and reinforcers of self. Heterosexual feminists have, too, throughout the ages, drawn strength from their friendships with women, from chosen celibacy, or from the separation of sex from love.

It is not through a mythology of bonding that we know of this sisterhood. It is through diaries and letters that the bond is expressed. Historian Nancy Cott studied the diaries of 100 women living in New England from 1780 to 1835. She found that although their roles were not equal to men's, they dominated the domestic sphere by choice, all but excluding men. Their subjugation by the patriarchy forced them to depend on one another for "emotional expression and security." Similar affection was not expressed with men because "they were not regarded as peers of men."

During the seventeenth and eighteenth centuries, pairs of traveling Quaker women ministers shared the hardships of separation from their families while living in the wilderness or, frequently, in prison, where they endured beatings. The history of feminism and antislavery is full of women's friendships. The best known is the long friendship among Elizabeth Cady Stanton, Lucretia Mott and Susan B. Anthony.

During the nineteenth century, although marriages became somewhat more equal, husbands still did not offer emotional support to their wives. Women continued to depend on other women. And, as recent research has proven, women's organizations were responsible for bringing libraries, beauty and order to towns and cities. Historian Carol Smith-Rosenberg concludes that American women's lives were organized around a network of women's friendships which sustained their devotion to husbands and family. There was a constant flow of letters, visiting and mutual assistance.

As our society became more mobile these intimacies decreased. Women speak of their families and friends living in different parts of the country. They spend time and money on the telephone, much like our Iranian, Dr. Abgahari, in the last chapter, talking to friends in other cities. Many women observe that they don't have time to make friends. Obligations to work, household management, family or partner do not leave time for nurturing friendships.

No Time For Friendship

No time for friendship and little time for companionship. . . . Women and men may be approaching one another on a more egalitarian basis these days but they have precious little time to explore and reconcile their "cultural" differences. It is their different experience with friendship that we are trying to understand here. It becomes a question of survival.

As Lerner concludes:

> The system of patriarchy is a historic construct; it has a beginning; it will have an end. Its time seems to have nearly run its course — it no longer serves the needs of men or women and in its inextricable linkage to militarism, hierarchy and racism it threatens the very existence of life on earth.

It is imperative that we open up to each other, without judgment or criticism, learning each other's language, values and expectations about friendship.

The Ghost Of Mother

According to Eichenbaum and Orbach, some women seek the same relationships with their friends that they had with their mothers. If men's problems with their lives begin with an early and ambiguous separation from mother, women have the opposite problem. They tend to search for the "merged attachment" with surrogate mothers. The authors say:

> In adult relationships, she is searching to find herself. But because the only mechanism she has for doing so is through merging and identifying with others, she comes to these relationships with emotional malleability. She comes with her emotional antennae ready to tune into the needs of the other. She is ready to adjust herself, deny herself, indeed lose herself [in order to find herself] in the attachment. But this process means that she loses sight of her own separate needs and desires. A search begins to find them in the other. She may no longer know what she wants in a clear way and looks to the other to provide an answer. . . . Thus relations based on merger mean that often women are bound to one another in a restricting way. Without realizing it, in bonding together to find strength, they can feel severely limited.

This twisted mother/daughter relationship is not as common as we are led to believe, according to Terri Apter. Fighting with Mom is a sign of attachment, not of separation. Apter interviewed 65 mother/daughter pairs. She did not find the animosity Eichenbaum and Orbach suggest. She says, "The aim of the argument was never to separate; it was always characterized by the underlying demand, 'See me as I am, and love me for what I am.'" Daughters are looking for individuation, not divorce — a severing of affection. However, such confrontation scares men.

Consider how one novelist views the mother/daughter tie:

> We want to please our mothers, emulate them, disgrace them, oblige them, outrage them and bury ourselves in the mysteries and consolations of their presence. When my mother and I are in the same room, we work magic on each other: I grow impossibly cheerful and am guilty of re-imagined naivete and other indulgent stunts, and my mother's sad helpless dithering becomes a song of succor. Within minutes, we're pedaling away, the two of us, a genetic sewing machine that runs on limitless love. It's my belief that be-

tween mothers and daughters there is a kind of blood-hyphen that is, finally, indissoluble.

As we have said, the family experience prepares the girl for friendships. Judith Salsman reported a group of girls in a private school whose friendships were problematic. Seven of the nine had experienced a high conflict divorce between their parents with alienation from their father. Eight of the nine used avoidance to cope with friendships. Salsman predicts poor adult relationships:

> As a result, these girls face the prospect of entering adult attachments without having practiced certain skills within family attachments. In particular, they lack experience with expressing their own wishes within attachment and having these wishes honored if not granted. Moreover, they have missed out on opportunities to develop strategies for conflict resolution other than the habit of silencing oneself or turning away from conflict altogether.

A Smattering Of Models

Models for women's friendships may be found in the following novels (recommended by Pogrebin): Francine du Plessix Gray, *World Without End;* Gail Godwin, *The Finishing School;* Alice Walker, *The Color Purple;* Gloria Naylor, *The Women of Brewster Place;* Joyce Carol Otates, *Solstice;* Faye Weldon, *Female Friends;* Toni Morrison, *Sula;* Elizabeth Benedict, *Slow Dancing;* Marge Piercy, *Small Changes* and Joan Didion, *Book of Common Prayer.*

It may be noted that the theme of several of these books is women's bonding through adversity surrounding men. While adversity is a common bonding theme for men, men's friendship novels usually use other elements as the goad — natural calamity or danger, sports, war.

A controversial film illustrated this theme. *Thelma and Louise* (1991) escape a loutish husband only to kill another lout because of an attempted rape, rob a store and blow up a harassing truck driver's rig, among other plot twists. Much like a typical male "road-buddy" film, this one is remarkable for portraying women as kick-ass rebels.

There have been other films in the past which dwelt on women's friendships, where men were an important influence on the relationship. The Nazis came between Jane Fonda and Vanessa Redgrave in *Julia* (1977). Anne Bancroft and Shirley MacLaine continue their estrangment over MacLaine's husband in *The Turning Point*. Without the physical presence of one man, men still influence Clare Boothe Luce's *The Women* (1939), a gross stereotype of divorcing women. *The Group* chronicles the soap-opera lives of eight Vassar graduates.

Some films suggest a lesbian relationship, or the suspicion of one, as in the French *Entre Nous* (1982) and the earlier film and play by Lillian Hellman, *The Children's Hour*. Mariel Hemingway tackles an erotic relationship between female athletes in *Personal Best* (1982). *Desert Hearts* (1987) has an even more explicit lesbian theme.

Conversely, I could hardly list all the male-buddy friendship films, even if I left out all the war and cowboy movies. In only a small percentage do women represent an adversary for the men. Homosexual themes are even less prominent.

Competition

Women have always competed with one another — for men. Now they compete with women and men for jobs, promotions and status. A recent book by Judith Briles documents the sabotage many women have experienced in the workplace. Tara Roth Madden's book, *Women Versus Women: The Uncivil Business War*, describes the same theme.

Women are confronted with a new environment to which they are trying to adjust. Some adjust by taking on the competitive style of men in business. Some drop out to find more congenial avenues for their creativity. A few bring a woman's culture to the corporate jungle. One survey found that only 175 (2.6 percent) of the 6,502 Fortune 500 officers were women. The "glass ceiling," old-boy networks and a later entry into the corporate world are blamed.

There is another reason. Many women dropped out of the greedy narcissism of the '80s to pursue more ethically compatible careers. I hope that some of the corporate survivors bring a woman's consciousness to the boardrooms. It would be a tragedy if women have to behave like men to become CEOs. We have seen in Chapter 6 that workaholism is a lonely addiction with un-healthy consequences. Obsession with work exacerbates the dif-ficulties men have in making friends with men. Women in the same conditions report the same phenomenon. Perhaps they will learn from men's experience that the corporate ladder is not worth the price of friendlessness.

Eva Margolies blames Mom for keeping women from being good competitors. She translates a fear of competitive rivalry be-tween daughter and mother to the daughter's lack of competitive desire in the business world. Are we continuing to judge women by men's standards? Hollywood has already tried to answer the question in the films *9 to 5* (1980) and *Working Girl* (1989).

Five Women, Class Of '69

In March 1991, five women converged on Naples, Florida, for their tri-annual reunion. I asked one of them, Karen, to describe their friendship. Although none of them could easily afford the trip, they had to celebrate their turning 40 together. All had been close friends since grade school, two since kindergarten.

Karen says, "I can't describe the commitment we have for one another . . . but we all made that trip in spite of our finances. I had just spent two years getting my teaching degree and I was strapped. The others were in a similar situation for one reason or another. But we all made it. It's just amazing.

"I really can't explain what keeps us together," Karen offers. "I don't even remember what brought us back together in the late '70s. But when we got together, we decided to have a reunion every three years, no husbands, no kids . . .

"We had fights and falling-outs in high school. I think girls can be really vicious to one another. But it was never four against one. Carla was my closest friend and she was close friends with Doris, who lived in the same neighborhood. Mary and I are the tallest so we were always in the back of the classroom. Pauline was added in first grade because she was a close friend of Mary's. I went to a different school during grades six through eight but we still got together, the five of us. I went to France during my senior year, but we always kept in touch. Then we split up to go to different colleges, got married and so on . . . a period of seven to ten years when we didn't get together.

"Now it's our common history which keeps us together. The unique thing is that we are all Catholics. The Catholic Church in our suburb was the predominant institution. We all grew up in Catholic schools. That was in the '60s, with Catholic discipline and Catechism, and the Vietnam War and drugs . . . you know?

"When we get together, we talk about our husbands and children and divorce and family. And being single — there are two of us who are single again. It's like group therapy. Last time I told them about a problem I am having with my brother. Then Mary cried about her sister. We didn't give any advice to each other, just support.

"The lines of communication aren't equal. I live the farthest away. I call Carla all the time but just send Doris a Christmas card. But when we get back together, we all feel like we just saw each other yesterday. There's actually no strangeness. The friendship keeps changing. It's dynamic in the lines of communication. Sometimes it's Mary and I, then Carla or Pauline may confide in me.

"What holds us together? I really can't put it into words. We found out several years ago that we were all from dysfunctional families. I told them about my experience with Al-Anon. Then the others described their families. Oh, I think we sensed what was going on in the families, but we never talked about it. There was something in the Catholic education that really made us think. It was a good education, but it was also traumatic.

"Going through all those hard times during puberty there was always someone to talk to. When I was in college, I had cancer, and it looked like I would die. My dysfunctional family — I'm the fourth of seven children, right in the middle — couldn't handle it. But my four friends kept visiting me in the hospital and joking, trying to keep my spirits up.

"No one knows me any better than they do. I don't have to prove anything. All the tension happened in high school. Now we joke about our getting flabby and fat. We had a good laugh about ourselves in our bathing suits."

I asked Karen if her friendships with males were different. "I've had a close friendship with a former male colleague of 18 years ago. But we couldn't see each other for a long time because my husband was so jealous. We had terrible fights about it and, interestingly, he was the one who broke up our marriage by being unfaithful.

"Yes, I am able to have equally intimate relationships with men. I just don't have the opportunity. The friendship doesn't seem any different than with my women friends. We share the same things. I guess it's because I've learned to be so open in recovery."

Karen spent several years in a "power" company finding clients. "I was making big bucks and I hated it." She started back to school to change careers before her boss gave her an ultimatum: Either move to another market or be fired. She chose to finish her education for a new career.

"I'm much happier now, although I'm earning about the same as I did ten years ago. It was worth taking that financial cut to have peace of mind. My life now is very spiritually based. I think there are a lot of women out there trying to compete with men but I think you'll only be happy when you find peace in yourself. You're not going to change the world. Find your peace in just doing the next right thing.

"I guess I learned about friendship from my older brother and sister. My father was an alcoholic, and my mother was too busy with three other children younger than me. So my brother and sister actually raised me."

Karen summarizes her philosophy: "There are two ways to wake up each morning. One is with fear, the other is with love. I choose love."

Questions

- Who are your models of women's friendship?
- How has adversity shaped your friendships?
- How has your mother affected your relationships?

CHAPTER · TEN

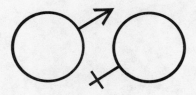

Rapprochement:
Men And Women
Can Be Friends

— ✳ —

*In love, we can hate
the person we love. . . . In friendship,
there is no room for hate.*

— Francesco Alberoni

Every day there are more reasons for men and women to learn how to make friends with the other sex.

In this rapidly changing world, men and women are increasingly thrown together in their daily lives, and opportunities to make friends abound. However, at times it seems as if the gain is not worth the effort, the embarrassment or the fear of rejection when we attempt to initiate a friendship dance with the other sex.

Among the younger generations who have experienced the rising equal treatment of women, social communication appears easier. Young men have seen their sisters excel in areas traditionally reserved for males. But since most members of society are still struggling with the notion of equality in economic and political power, relationships between men and women may resemble an uneasy truce in "the longest war" more than friendship.

New models and behaviors are necessary for friendly attachments between men and women to flourish. Models of same-sex friendships, which we have seen in previous chapters, will not transfer to friendships between the sexes. Each person must learn how he or she is different from the other sex: in expectations, in vocabulary and how words are used, and in styles of relating. In the dance of life, the opportunity for male/female friendship opens up a whole new resource for assuaging our loneliness.

Another factor that makes learning about cross-sex friendships timely is the increasing number of sexual harassment claims. Instead of viewing women in the workplace as fair game for sexual "kidding around," the safer avenue is to make friends. And a man approached by a co-worker in a friendly manner should not assume she is "after" him. The alternative to violating physical and emotional boundaries is to treat co-workers as equals — a prerequisite for friendship.

The worldwide AIDS epidemic should make us all aware that casual sex in friendship, courtship or marriage is life threatening. Alarming statistics indicate that heterosexual transmission of HIV, the virus that causes AIDS, is increasing at a rapid rate, and the number of women infected is expected to match the number of men by the turn of the century in the United States, as it already has in other countries. The trail of clothes leading to the bedroom depicting passionate, casual sex in so many recent films is a dangerous out-dated message which is fatally irresponsible.

Among informed populations, the idea of becoming friends first, really getting to know and trust that person of the other sex before engaging in sexual activity is changing the rules of dating. In the process, it is opening up the possibilities of cross-sex friendship as an end in itself. Even in long-term marriages, the friendship factor is what will enable partners to frankly discuss possibilities that either has engaged in risky behaviors during the last ten years. The long incubation period for AIDS means that the virus can live in your body unnoticed for years. Part of a loving commitment is to be tested for HIV antibodies.

Alarmingly, the fear of AIDS has not significantly changed risky behaviors among those infected or uninfected. A 20-something author writing in *Psychology Today* concludes that:

> We're still having sex, but we're afraid of it, too. We are talking about it differently — confessing our pasts but lying about our presents — the underground of sexual adventure has become a dangerous sex casino where love, lies and fear are a perpetual threesome in the bedroom of America.

There are other reasons for having cross-sex friends: they offer their unique perspective on our world. Different humor. Different quantities of self-confidence and vulnerability. There is so much more than sex that we can give and take in a cross-cultural friendship. While the same sex might provide comfort in shared feelings, experiences or anxieties, the other sex can provide the seasoning which comes from a slightly different set of feelings, experiences and anxieties. The chemistry has frequently been explosive, but it holds the potential for exciting new creations.

Cross-sex friendship is an idea whose time has come, but there are many barriers to getting beyond sex-role stereotypes, old prejudices, fears and habits of the mind.

Cross-Sex Barriers

I asked participants in a workshop to brainstorm barriers to cross-sex friendships. The answers they gave were serious but frequently were accompanied by explosions of nervous laughter, indicating that even talking about barriers was embarrassing:

"Suspicion of sex. Is this supposed to be sex or is it not supposed to be sex? You've got bona fide sex and you've got is it or isn't it sex."

"How about jealousy?"

"Different interests."

"Stigma . . . societal stigma."

"You mean societal expectations? Society looks at cross-sex friendships with some suspicion. 'Is this just a friendship?' "

"Behaviors? Not being aware of the difference between men and women."

"Being married as a social barrier. You know, you're limited to your spouse's married friends."

"Right. And in marriage is this person supposed to be my *all* of the opposite sex?"

"Men can be confused in what they want. On an intellectual level they can say, 'Hey, let's keep this on a friendship basis.' and emotionally, 'Gee, I'd sure like to go to bed with her.' "

"That's typical for women too."

"There's the difference between what I want, what I think I want and how to tell the difference . . ."

"There are some things that men are interested in and some things women are interested in and when you find something that is shared, that's the basis for good cross-sex friendship. There are some women that I kayak with and that's a very good basis for a relationship."

"Peer pressure makes friendship difficult. Say you go out to a movie together. A friend asks, 'Are you dating now?' "

"Look what we ask of men. We ask men to be sensitive, under-standing, to join in groups, to talk with us but we wonder about them as soon as they do."

"Men have a corresponding script in that they want women to be strong and independent and self-sufficient in a 'feminine' and dependent way."

These workshop participants were defining for themselves what they expected in cross-sex friendships/partnerships. It appears that everything we do with someone of the other sex is thought to have sexual implications. One survey found that sex is inferred on television about every four minutes. The media knows how to get our attention. Maybe if we admit that sexual fantasies are embedded in our culture due to all the advertising and media exposure, we can get past the hype to what is more important.

Harvey Jackins, the originator of re-evaluation counseling, has discovered through working with thousands of clients, that adults need very little sex. We are looking for touch. Remember that fantasies don't have to be acted upon. We can even learn to talk about them as a way of discharging all that anxiety and embarrassment.

How Do We Talk About
The Fear Of Or Hope For Sex?

The fear of or hope for sex are significant barriers to cross-sex friendships as we have heard from the workshop attendees. When a man and a women meet, unless they are totally inappropriate for each other — sometimes even if they are — the question of sex comes to mind and makes for an uneasy truce.

Does talking about it help or hurt? Some people feel that getting it out into the open defuses the feelings. For example, Jan and I spent some very emotional afternoons together in a group of hospice volunteers. The two of us began to meet afterward just to talk, to come down from the emotions involved in dying.

At the second meeting she asked, "What do you want to happen between us?"

I had never experienced such directness before and was stopped for a moment. Then I answered, "To be friends." The relief on her face was obvious. We continued to meet until one of us ended our hospice work. While our meetings became less frequent, we did celebrate together at times.

When my partner ended our relationship with devastating abruptness, I told Jan and she invited me to breakfast at her new home. Something was now different between us. I wanted her and I respected our agreement. Instead of talking about it, I stopped calling her. I know that all I wanted was to be held for a while but I couldn't say it. The pain of that separation remains and not being able to tell her haunts me.

On the other hand, one of the men in the brainstorming sessions said, "There is an opposite tack. Approach the relationship the way you want it to be and assume the other person will do likewise." He was attacked immediately by two women who described painful experiences caused by assuming instead of talking.

Of course, clearing the air for one by admitting there is an attraction that is not going to be acted upon may be exciting for the other by initiating a fantasy. In treating a cross-sex relationship as a nonsexual friendship, some may not say it but mean it by their behavior. On the opposite side, some may say it and not mean it. Friendship is no easy thing to achieve when the chemistry of attraction is involved. In fact, it may be the *most* difficult alternative.

In *Notes To Myself*, Hugh Prather explores various aspects of being open and honest in the face of a powerful attraction:

> If my sexual desire for a woman is so strong and so persistent that it's getting in the way of my communication with her, I might do her and me a favor by telling her so . . . this approach, however, requires that I be deeply honest with myself about my motives because so often when sex is mentioned, people think they are being asked to do something. Therefore to bring this subject up can easily become not an exercise in openness but a deceitful manipulation . . .

Models Of Cross-Sex Communication

Between Individuals

A *marriage*, particularly a modern marriage, cannot last long without friendship. The passion and eroticism must be balanced with friendship and caring. As the marriage goes through its various stages of approach and distancing, the ability and willingness to talk keeps the attachment from becoming unglued. At the same time, a stable marriage allows outside friendships without jealousy.

It is not that stable marriages do not have their conflicts; it is that conflict can be talked about, confronted honestly in spite of all the anxiety. Sometimes safe communication must be learned. Just as we saw in Chapter 4 that "I" messages which convey emotions are better than accusing another, in marriage we learn to feed back the other's emotions, to validate them and to empathize *even if we think the feelings are not warranted*.

Summarizing her 40-year marriage, author Madeleine L'Engle writes, "I do not think that death can take away the fact that Hugh and I are 'we' and 'us,' a new creature born at the time of our marriage vows, which has grown along with us as our marriage has grown. Even during the times, inevitable in all marriages, when I have felt angry or alientated, the instinctive 'we' remains." In both sexual and nonsexual relationships we strive for the "we of friendship" — interdependence.

Interdependence

Past relationships between men and women have been judged as complementary. This assigned gender role to men and women viewed the joining as some kind of completed model. Such reasoning inferred that men and women were not complete by themselves. There are some very ancient myths that men and women were once complete, were separated and now are attempting to rejoin when they couple.

Interdependence — the last stage in the development of friendship — does not imply the complementarity described above. At the point where we accept ourselves as whole people, unique, valid, authentic, we are ready to accept others as equals. We then can recognize that others are not here to complete us but to enhance us. The interaction of two (or more) souls creates more than the sum of the parts. This is the mystical experience so many have sought and so few have found.

The best model of interdependence is still friendship. For friendship continues to be less a goal than a process. As the friends continue to develop emotionally and spiritually, the interdependence will have the opportunity to mature and create new facets of affinity.

The Workplace is another opportunity to experience interdependence. Two investigators of cross-sex friendships within the workplace have compared this relationship to courtship. The pair is intimate in private situations; the two make dates, eat together and drink toasts together after their successes; they may travel together and share common excitements. *Such relationships work only if the boundaries are agreed on.* The frightening conversation about expectations must be initiated before a lot of eggs are broken.

The benefits of cross-sex friendships in the workplace or in clubs, volunteer organizations and religious groups are high when communication is honest. The process . . .

1. Discovers new ways of relating to the other sex
2. Directs the usual sexual energy to creative energy
3. Models this new way of relating for others to emulate
4. Enriches self-discovery, including enhancing the primary companionship. The worst thing you can do is not talk about the relationship.

The women in the brainstorming session knew the dangers of workplace romances. One admitted, "I want a good working relationship. I've fallen into the wrong trap. There's a thin narrow line crossing that line — we all know it. How do we deal with our feelings?"

Another added, "You don't get a charge [romance] out of work. You don't let go [of control] if it's a good working relationship. You hold back. And that's okay."

One married woman whose husband was present said, "I couldn't go home and talk to Emmett about my job and not talk about a work relationship."

Sey Chassler, a former editor of *Redbook*, describes his feelings of camaraderie with his female co-workers:

> They were like the feelings of a locker room after a game played hard and won. They felt like sweat. They felt like heroism. . . . How marvelous to feel that way about a woman and not want to go to bed with her. Perhaps in prehistory, when female and male hunted and gathered side-by-side, similar feelings occurred.

Notice how Chassler uses male sports images to describe his experience. He separates his erotic feelings from sexual ones. That is what I failed to do with Jan and what most men and women fail to do when they feel the attractive chemistry working. Both sexes can learn to ask themselves the same question Jan asked me, "What do you want to happen?"

What happens when a work friendship turns on you suddenly? "Dear Abby" recently ran a letter from a single woman complaining that her five-year-friendship with a married colleague was jeopardized when he propositioned her with the suggestion of drinks and a hotel room. After her silent refusal, she asked Abby, "Is it okay to become closer platonic friends? I'd like to know him better. I could learn a lot from him." Abby missed a great opportunity when she answered, ". . . All he wants is a few hours of sex . . . there is no way you can have an intimate nonsexual relationship with this man."

They already had five years of friendship with no propositions. Why throw all of this energy away? All she had to say to him was, "These are the boundaries. I would like you as a platonic friend. I have a lot to learn from you and sex is not one of those things."

The *mentor relationship* offers still another form of friendship, although it is almost a given that at some point the unequal relationship must be severed. Mentorship is much like raising adolescents, knowing they must leave home eventually so that they can visit later as adults. During their middle years, emotionally secure men and women experience their sense of the flow of the generations, their generativity and reach back to assist younger associates.

Cross-sex mentorships are more tentative since the power is so easily abused or manipulated sexually. However, great productivity and advancement have come from male/female mentorship where either sex may have more power. Just as in families, the power difference must not be abused.

Frank was Alise's boss and mentor. She thought he was a great model as a man who had risen to be a partner in his law firm. She was a new lawyer near the top of her class. For the first year he guided her through the minefields of corporate law in a prestigious firm. One day he left his desk to come sit beside her on the leather couch in his office. His right leg rubbed against hers. When she moved, he followed and began telling a dirty joke. She was too shocked to say anything and left as soon as she could.

The next day she found an opportunity to say, "You have been my mentor and I really appreciate the attention you have given my professional growth. I was very uneasy yesterday when you invaded my personal space and told an inappropriate story. I don't want to lose our working relationship. But I will tell you immediately when I feel uncomfortable that way again."

After a rather amiable six months, Frank came upon her from behind and began rubbing her shoulders while telling her of one of his sexual exploits with a former secretary. She turned away and said, "That's inappropriate. And we were doing so well together." After a third episode she took a sexual harassment complaint to the executive officer of the company. Frank was reprimanded and she was reassigned to one of the female partners.

What do you suppose the outcome might have been if Anita Hill had felt safe enough to confront Clarence Thomas in a similar manner?

Gay men and straight women frequently find an asexual common ground. Both are able to be comfortable with one another because the boundaries are clear.

In Groups

Every time I present a workshop I learn one thing over again: how revealing to the other sex it is when men or women talk about their feelings with one another. It reinforces the observation, which Harriet Goldhor Lerner also recognizes in *The Dance of Intimacy,* that we are really dealing with two different cultures. Generally when men and women are together, there is so much posturing that real exchange of emotions never takes place.

To set the environment up so men and women have a better opportunity to be honest, first I separate them. Then I ask each sex to respond to questions. One provocative question which always leads to a heated response is, "What are some questions you would like to ask the other sex but are afraid to?"

Once the questions or responses are written, I ask both sexes to come back together in two concentric circles. The gender in the middle tightens up and responds to the question from the other sex as if those on the outside were not there. Those on the outside remain silent. That's the hardest part.

When the inner group is through, they change places with the outer group. The new inner group first has an opportunity to respond to what they have just heard. Then they can answer the questions submitted by the other group. Finally, one big circle is formed and the question is asked, "What did you learn from doing this?"

Having been "a fly on the wall" in many of these groups, I have felt the raw anger, frustration and caretaking expressed by the women, and the anxiety, frustration and fear shared by the men. But in the end, along with the relief that it wasn't as fearful as anticipated, there was an increased understanding of the other sex.

I have led workshops to form men's self-led support groups for over 15 years. These consist of six to a dozen men who want a safe place to talk about their lives. The ground rules are simple: commitment to the process, confidentiality, listening rather than trying to fix things, sharing feelings and honesty. I also have my own support group where I can be totally honest and not fear judgment. During these years the men have shared some of their most profound anxieties, embarrassments and fears. Just talking about them has helped and taught us that we are not alone.

Some women have similar support groups. My partner missed her circle of friends upon her return from California several years ago and recently joined one rising out of one of my Friendship Workshops. Such groups are safe places to discharge anxieties and role play talking about scary things.

When the subject of sex comes up in the workshops, a lot of emotional discharge takes place first: the jokes, the one-liners, the laughing and snickering. So how do we talk about our boundaries with our cross-sex friends in this frightening, emotionally charged environment? How do you get past the anticipated embarrassment of explaining your sexual boundaries?

12-Step Resources

If you don't have friends or support groups in which you can role play, 12-Step programs are good models. In 12-Step groups men and women share their deepest secrets in an atmosphere of mutual support and trust. Fellowship is one of the main components of recovery, and enduring fellowship in a group frequently leads to strong same-sex and cross-sex friendships. Members of Alcoholics Anonymous like to socialize with one another, and find it easier to maintain sobriety with friends who don't drink. Mutual support in a common cause is a strong motive to moving beyond the usual barriers to friendship.

In another 12-Step group, Sex and Love Addicts Anonymous (SLAA), men and women support one another in periods of sexual abstinence. SLAA members learn that those to whom they are instantly attracted are usually the worst possible choices of partners. Remember we described these potentially addictive chemical rushes in Chapter 2. SLAA members call such encounters "adrenaline rushes" or "sexual fixes" and avoid them until they learn other ways to relate. Building partnerships is a strong theme in this group, as is self-honesty. Rich cross-sex friendships are formed, based on mutual understanding and respect for another's process of change.

Such groups, even if not joined, are models for group work where men and women can learn to be friends.

The Embarrassment Factor

How do we learn to talk about something we find so embarrassing? First ask yourself what do you want to happen?

If you are honest, you will find there is a part of you which sees sex as an affirmation of your attractiveness. Get past that narcissism to what really attracts you to the other. Humor? Self-confidence? Vulnerability? Similarity? Intelligence? Uniqueness? There is so much more than sex that we can give and take in a cross-cultural friendship.

- I want to be able to share my insides, my feelings and fantasies without judgment.
- I want to hug you when you are down and be able to ask for hugs when I am the same.
- I want to celebrate your happy times and let you in on mine.
- I want to see the world through your eyes and mind.
- I want us to be friends.

Once you have decided to make friends with a member of the other sex, it's time to talk to them about it. Set up the discussion as to time, place and script as if it were any other important communication in your life. Try out several scripts.

For example, "I am really attracted to your happy personality, your humor, your intensity and caring about others and I would like to be friends. I am concerned that this attraction might be taken as sexual and I don't want that. We can enjoy each other's company and share our time and interests."

If It Works So Well, Why Don't We Talk About It More Often?

Because we are scared. We are afraid that our feelings will be rejected. That hurts. Remember that the most important technique in communication is the art of listening. When we feel that we are not heard, we experience rejection. Our emotional core is denied. There is a good chance that we experienced a lot of not being heard before our adulthood.

This rejection can occur when the other person disclaims our sentiments. When he or she says to you, "I don't know where you got such a crazy idea," that is an emotional put-down.

It hurts just as much when the other laughs at the vulnerability you have just expressed. It becomes much easier to hide our feelings and hope that the dance of attachment will somehow work out.

We are afraid of being shamed. Most of us are carrying around feelings of shame and embarrassment from the past. These stifle spontaneity in our present. When we speak of anything which we learned was shameful, such as having feelings or talking about sex, we blush, sweat, our palms become clammy and we giggle nervously.

It appears easier to retreat, to become shy, rather than go through such emotional contortions. Some people are born shy and, for others, shyness is another manifestation of shame.

According to John Bradshaw,

> Shyness is a natural boundary which guards us from being exposed or wounded by a stranger. Many of us feel shy when we are faced with the prospect of walking up to a stranger. We feel self-conscious, we stammer in speech or speak in an awkward manner. This may trigger embarrassment.
>
> We are born uninhibited in expressing our feelings. As boys we learn by peer and parental put-downs not to express our vulnerability. As girls we learn not to express our sexuality. *Instead of learning that feelings don't have to be acted on, we learn to deny them.* It is time to learn a new script.

Getting Help Getting Past The Embarrassment

Clearness

The Quakers (Religious Society of Friends) have developed a process for helping people make decisions and work through problems called clearness. It works with any group willing to listen and follow the simple rules. The person wishing clearness calls a few friends together. If one person is having some conflict with another, both ask friends to attend. One friend acts as a facilitator explaining the process, setting the agenda and helping the meeting to flow. First, the problem is stated. In this case it might be something like, "How do I tell Sandy I want to be a friend and not a lover? I can't seem to find the right time or the right words." The people are there to listen and feed back, to support the emotions, to raise questions, to suggest options and to offer continuing support.

Re-evaluation Counseling (RC)

A group with a direct remedy for embarrassment is RC, headquartered in Seattle. RC theory states, in brief, that human beings are naturally intelligent and capable of making completely rational choices. But our intelligence is occluded by psychological distress patterns which shut down our clarity of mind and free attention. When our free attention is shut down, our distress patterns take over, and we act "in pattern," predictably making less-than-the-best choices. When allowed to discharge our distress, we regain enough free attention to make rational choices.

The distress of embarrassment is discharged by talking about the distressing topic, laughing nervously, sweating and yawning in the presence of those who focus loving attention on us and who do not judge or interfere with our discharge process. RC groups are available in many communities as an option. Even without a group to work with, if you know that embarrassment can be diminished by talking and laughing through the scary material, you and a friend (*not* the person you're attracted to) can do some co-counseling together. This is a good way to rehearse what you know you must say but are too afraid to try.

Tell your friend over and over again and laugh all you need to until you no longer feel embarrassed. Your friend silently accepts everything you do and say. Know that it's okay to feel sexually attracted to someone and to be nervous and silly about it. Feelings are just feelings and they'll diminish in power if you discharge the patterns that hold them in place.

Can Men And Women Just Be Friends?

Most of my workshop attendees have seen the classic film *When Harry Met Sally* at least once. The film follows Harry and Sally from an initial sexual proposition and refusal, through a budding friendship to the love of the special qualities of the friend. When Harry responds to Sally's, "We are just going to be friends," with, "Men and women can't be friends because the sex thing gets in the way . . . no man can be friends with a woman that he finds attractive; he always wants to have sex with her," the friendship appears over. Attendees talk about the boundaries and the process the friendship takes before the real reasons for the mutual attraction surface. He loves all the unique little things about her. She responds with love in her eyes, "I really hate you, Harry." When he asks what Auld Lang Syne means, she responds, "It's about Old Friends."

Defining The Boundaries

Talking about it sets the boundaries. The psychologic process during growing up is one of learning ego boundaries: separating self and not-self. As adults we balance enclosure (protecting ourselves) and intrusion (letting others in). Our interiors are permeable but must be selectively so. We must feel comfortable with the intrusion.

So we set the parameters of friendship by how much intrusion we will allow. Isn't it better to make our boundaries clear? Only those who desire something other than friendship thrive on the ambiguity of sexual relations.

Talking about it may not always give the results desired. And yet not talking about it creates a poisonous underground fungus capable of destroying human relationships of all kinds. During our childhoods, we learned that it was often easier to accuse, blame, shout, fight or run away than to communicate. Some schools are teaching communication skills in order to reduce the violence in the classroom. As adults we had better learn that the mature path toward resolving conflict, making friends and finding life partners is *talking about it*.

Boundary Questions:

The recent hurricane of recovery and relationship information is not the result of new family dynamics as much as the recognition that many of the old family dynamics are emotionally destructive, tearing down the ego-barriers. Breached boundaries need to be repaired before the self is confident to make friends.

- Whom do you attract? What kind of acquaintances call on you? Are they needy? Are they available to you when you want support?

- Can you say no? How does it make you feel? Anxious?
- Do you apologize when setting boundaries?
- Does your no mean maybe, sometimes? How direct are your statements?

Artist and therapist Sue Bender has shared her experience learning how to simplify and set boundaries in *Plain and Simple: A Woman's Journey to the Amish*. She found her spiritual journey intimately involved in her work and required leaving space for herself. But setting boundaries with some acquaintances caused them to pull away. As she worked on her book she found a community of friends surrounding her.

> What happened was a laying on of hands — a handmade process — a procession of friendship. Friends, one more busy than the next, came, reached out beyond their overcrowded schedules, saw the possibilities and offered their help. This group of strong-minded individuals joined forces — cooperated. It wasn't the Amish way of community but I saw these friends as a community of quilters, making the quilt stronger, more mine than I could have done alone.

Setting boundaries created real interdependent friendships.

Other Barriers

Among the barriers to cross-sex friendships raised by the workshop members, jealousy, exclusivity, social expectations and assumptions stand out. Jealousy as a fear of abandonment has been examined in Chapter 5. The expectation that a marriage will fulfill all of the needs of both partners is a common myth. As the natural distancing occurs after the initial intense joining, frictions occur over friendships outside of the couple. These anxieties must be talked about too. Cross-sex friendships between married and single men and women will not mature unless all those involved feel comfortable with the boundaries.

A man and woman together are assumed to be joined or dating in this culture. In any developing cross-sex friendship the feelings of the friends about such an assumption should be explored too. Responses to "Are you dating now?" should be role played: Something like "John is more than a date, he is a friend" will give people something to think about. There is no such thing as "Just friends." One workshop attendee wrote, "A good friendship is a miracle."

When men and women listen to one another in my workshops or other safe environments, they begin to realize the slight but important cultural differences between the sexes. If we want to communicate with this other culture, we need act like social anthropologists. As Homa or Woma we need to learn the other's language and styles of communication. Then we can listen to their stories and understand their anxieties, their hopes and their expectations. That is, understanding how the other culture frames its conversation helps in talking with them.

The Homa And The Woma

Look at these two cultures again for a moment. The Homa have grown up fearing and fascinated by the Woma. They fear the control they feel the Woma have over them and they are fascinated by the cultural differences, including their different bodies, their softness, their nurturing, their odors. Living as close as they do, they tend to believe that the Woma think the same way they do. The Homa seem to need daily assurance of their cultural identity. Success is their goal; status is their criterion. One measure of their status is their ability to possess a Woma. This possession only appears to satisfy their attachment needs. However, their attention span is quite short. As a culture they tend to confuse attachment with sex and use sex both as a symbol of success and as a source of emotional contact with the Woma.

In contrast, the Woma have grown up fearing and fascinated by the Homa. They fear the dominance expressed by the Homa in so many parts of their lives; they are fascinated by the cultural differences, including their different bodies, their strength, their aggressiveness, their ritual behaviors. They have learned to survive in the past under the domination of the Homa so they know more how to get around them, rather than communicate with them. The Woma are beginning to assert their own cultural power. Community is their goal; connection is their criterion. For many Woma, reproduction of their species is a strong attraction which satisfies some of their attachment needs. As a culture they enjoy sex as part of their emotional attachment to another.

Meeting In The Middle

As the two cultures, men and women, approach equality in economic and political power and in the workplace, friendships between men and women become possible. However, as we have seen, new models and behaviors are necessary for friendly attachments to prosper.

Dance is a good example of the two cultures meeting in the middle. Back in the mid-1940s and Mrs. Murphy's dancing class, nothing could be worse for a 10-year-old boy's fall Saturday afternoons than dancing class. The only consolation was that the rest of the gang was also scrubbed squeaky clean and huddled in the ballroom instead of the football field. In the middle of the room, boys and girls were paired off by height. We tentatively held the girls at arms' length and tried to follow Mrs. Murphy's instructions punctuated by her clacking castanets.

As the classes continued, the two lines disappeared. The boys were instructed how to bow and ask a girl to dance. Male and female roles were clearly defined. Men were in charge and risked the embarrassment of possible rejection. Women were passive and risked the embarrassment of not being asked.

Fast forward to junior high school. It is the same ballroom, but now the lights are as low as the chaperone will allow. The music playing is "Stardust." Boys stand, hands in pockets, huddled at one end of the room. Girls stand at the other end, trying to ignore the boys ogling them. The boys discuss the possibility of asking a girl to dance. Friends advise, "Go ahead, she likes you. See how she is looking at you." Crossing the middle of the floor to ask one of a group of girls to dance is like running through the World War II mine fields we have just seen at the movies. We, both sexes, learn early that if you want to dance, it is best to be going steady with someone, anyone. You don't dance with friends.

The music and the environment have changed over the years but the anxiety remains just as palpable. All of us, not just the boys, are carrying condoms now. The dance of life has become more frantic, more frightening. The old sex roles are gone. The myths about the other sex and the expectations of ourselves are still being re-examined. The major difference today is that if we don't TALK ABOUT IT, we end up playing Russian roulette with our lives.

Questions:

- Have you experienced a cross-sex friendship before? Did it end? Why? What could have been done to prevent its ending?
- How have you been trained to relate to the other sex? Are there some changes you could make in the behaviors?
- What things do you think you might do with a cross-sex friend?
- Could you manage a sexual relationship with someone and a cross-sex friendship with someone else?
- What image do you have of a "sensitive man," an "assertive woman"?
- With whom can you talk about sex in general or your sexuality in particular? Why is talking about sex embarrassing for you?
- When have you experienced the feeling of unity with another, a sense of "we"?

Once you have your boundaries in place, return to those expectations men and women had so much trouble agreeing on in the first chapter. How do they work in cross-sex friendships?

Commitment — Where does this friend stand in your priority list? Who else is affected by this change in your priorities?

Complicity — What values, beliefs, habits, pleasures do you share?

Courage — Can you talk about your conflicts and talk about them fairly?

Intimacy — Do you have a sense that emotions are shared?

Engagement — What thoughtful things do you do, unsolicited, for your friend? What does your friend do for you?

Relaxation — Can you hang out together without an agenda?

Acceptance — Can you accept your friend's differences?

CHAPTER ELEVEN

Next Steps, New Steps

———— ✳ ————

WEST GA. WM, 50, gentle, sensitive, educated, no bad habits, lonely, neglected, seeks attention from lonely WF 25-55.

— Atlanta Journal-Constitution

SWF seeks SBM for fun and games and companionship, 5′6″, 155, likes flowers and tequila. I'm lonely.

— Journal-Constitution

Making friends should come naturally. If it feels difficult, it is because we have learned some assumptions and behaviors which inhibit the natural process. Now it's time to do the work to overcome the barriers which we recognize we have raised. Clearly the work is worth it. We understand our basic need for attachments of all kinds. And we also are clear that good attachments allow space to be alone with ourselves. When the attachment feels secure, we aren't jealous of outside friendships; we don't cling to and engulf the other person.

Living seems to be a paradox of attachment and separation, a continuous process of change. If, as philosopher Chauncey D. Leake says, we are living "to be satisfied," then we are living the paradox that we will never be satisfied for long.

As infants we tried to be in a state of continuous satisfaction. When we were uncomfortable, we let the world know. As we matured, more of our waking state seemed to be unsatisfied. Infantile and juvenile methods of coping with dissatisfaction didn't work in the adult world. Now we learn how to make attachments or we go without and feel lonely. So we learn to enjoy the bliss of belonging only briefly. Storr says, "Perfect happiness, the oceanic feeling of complete harmony between inner and outer worlds [which we felt as a newborn], is only transiently possible." Friendships can increase those happy feelings.

Next Steps

I sat in the dark theater watching the credits roll by and allowing the tears to dry. Jessica Tandy's character in *Fried Green Tomatoes* had just said, "You reminded me of something . . . the most important thing in life is friendship."

Men and women attending a Friendship Workshop have the same emotion. Learning that we all need friends helps us get past the fear of making the effort to make friends. It gives us courage to seek friendship.

We can make the call.

We, men and women, are most alike in our fears and foibles even if sometimes we act as if we live in different worlds. We can talk to one another.

We can decide for ourselves what we can give and get from the different kinds of friendship available.

Determining What You Want

One of the last exercises I ask workshop attendees to do is to write a make-believe ad. If you were going to a singles dating service or a match-making service to make friendships, you would be asked to fill out a questionnaire. (One matchmaking service advertises: "Beautiful Women Do Not Go To Single Bars.") Even the most perfunctory questionnaire would ask something about you and more about whom you are looking for. Isn't it reasonable to ask the same thing of your friendships?

Most of the personals in the newspapers seek, overtly or covertly, a sexual relationship. Try writing an ad describing yourself as an interesting friend who is seeking the same. Remember you don't have to send the ad.

One workshop participant wrote:

> FRIENDSHIP WANTED — Nontraditional person caught in traditional roles seeks assorted people with interesting outlooks on life for socializing. Enjoy various activities ranging from the outdoors (camping, hiking, cycling) to the indoors (movies, dinners, board games).

Would you be interested in answering that ad? The person had identified him/herself and the interests which may be shared. Notice that the sex of the people is not mentioned.

Think about the kinds of friendships you may want or you may already have: gossiping friends, party friends, "doing" friends and confidants.

Gossiping Friends

Recall that gossiping is information exchange about what you value in others. Gossiping and griping are verbal stroking. It is being in touch at a superficial level of intimacy.

Charles and Irene have been friends for 20 years since they worked together at a state agency. Although they have separate lives now, one or the other calls frequently to check in. They share stories about former colleagues and bosses. They complain to each other about their jobs, their children, the economy, the government and race relations. However, neither shares his or her history with their sexual partners. The risk of vulnerability is limited.

Party Friends

Karen is the life of the party. She knows how to organize and host. Everyone has a good time when she is there. She works hard at her real estate sales and plays hard. Yet no one really knows her. She is divorced with no children. Her friends call her when they are having a party, but she has no one to go to the movies or to dinner with.

"Doing" Friends

This is a large category of special interest friends. People you know under one set of circumstances, such as exercising together, in the same office, neighbors, drinking buddies or sports buddies. Someone to go to the movies with. You may have a drink or snack with them after aerobics or after work; that is as far as it goes. These may be an untapped source of more intimate friends.

Confidants

These are the ones with whom you share your intimacies — your vulnerabilities. They are the ones you call in a crisis because you know they will be there for you. Sharing anxieties and frustrations has made the bonds strong. You take emotional risks with these friends. Confidants reach in to stroke our inner selves.

Getting Clear Who You Are

What do you enjoy doing alone? (You may want to reread Chapter 7.) Which of those activities can be shared with another person? Would you like to be able to share the anxieties which have been going around and around in your head with no exit and no resolution?

What old tapes are you playing in relationships? Where do they come from? Do you feel your needs were not met during childhood? What about those disasters during adolescence? What are your romantic fantasies?

Previous painful experiences during childhood or later need not prevent us from making friends now. Living past pain, once we recognize the source, inhibits friendship in the present. *But we are resilient.*

How about competition? Do you seek it or shy away from it? Were you competitive in high school, college? When do you feel as if you are a failure?

Does jealousy, homophobia or sexual desire get in the way of your relationships? Where do these tapes come from?

Now, write that ad! If you get stuck, get some help.

Getting Help

You may need help in getting clear what you want. Paradoxically, friends are the first resource for those of us who need to clarify our expectations or to look at new directions. Remember the "clearness" process of The Religious Society of Friends (Quakers) described in the last chapter.

If you don't feel comfortable asking friends, seek out a self-help group in the newspaper or from a national hot line number. Most of these are modeled on the 12-Step Program. If you find others with similar values and a hopeful, helpful attitude, stick with them. If not, keep searching. When you find help, be sure you aren't getting into another addiction.

You may want private counseling or therapy. There are so many different kinds you may have to shop for a while. A sensitive counselor will not try to fit clients into a program which doesn't work for them. Remember you are making a rather firm attachment with this other person as part of your therapy.

Your counselor may lead you to therapy groups. One positive effect of working in groups is that you discover, just as in the Friendship Workshops, that you are not alone in your feelings and in the ghosts in your life.

How To Meet Friends Or Partners

1. Carry a conversation starter such as a book or pamphlet, or wear an unusual T-shirt.
2. Carry a card with your name and number — not necessarily an address. Give it to people who interest you.
3. Be open to contact. Carry open body language. Don't hide behind books or newspapers.
4. Identify your barriers. Which of the barriers that we look at rang a bell? Try new behaviors to overcome them.
5. Renew old acquaintances. Which of your casual friends would you like to get to know better?
6. Don't try so hard, relax.
7. Role play real interactions with others; not fantasies. Practice communication skills. Remember the conversation starters — where you live, hobbies and interests, vacations, jobs.
8. Where are you comfortable going alone and what can you do alone? Check out your newspapers and free throwaways. They carry calendars with events for everyone but the most reclusive.
9. Walk a pet, go window shopping, check out bookstores, libraries, trade shows.
10. Check out your work setting for potential friends.
11. Have a nonsignificant party. Invite acquaintances to bring a friend not their partner (if they have one). I know of one such party that resulted in three marriages.

12. Go dancing. As I have said, dance is a metaphor for intimacy and passion.
13. Check out those large family gatherings — I mean the big weddings, bar mitzvahs, yes, even memorial services.
14. Join service, sports, or volunteer organizations. One of the nicest cross-sex friendships I had was developed during my hospice work. Scores of these organizations are listed in the paper. I met most of my dating partners in volunteer organizations. See a list of suggestions in Appendix 2.
15. Go to continuing education classes on something which interests you. Most colleges have evening credit and non-credit classes.
16. Check out various religious organizations even if you don't wish to belong. Many churches and synagogues have a wide range of groups meeting every night of the week.
17. Make the call you have been afraid to make. Role play it a little first. What do you say if you reach an answering machine? What if you don't?

New Steps

First, with pen and paper, make a list of all the things you might do to make a friend. Take your time. Some workshop participants can develop ten or more. Some are stuck on two or three. Check the list above for hints.

Once you have exhausted all possibilities, choose one, which you definitely, no hesitation, can do. Make a covenant with yourself to do it. You may have someone in mind to whom you could tell your plans. Whatever, *do it!*

Making friends takes time and energy. It takes the willingness to risk self-exposure, to accept ourselves as well as others. It requires thoughtfulness and the courage to express our feelings.

In two weeks go back to the list. Covenant to do another "reaching out" to make a friend.

In the frantic lives we lead, the four dimensions of loneliness become more evident. We must find time to make friends with confidants, to make friends with those we touch in our communities, to make friends with the diverse peoples of this earth because they have become our neighbors, and to make friends with the earth itself for our own spiritual well-being.

The benefits of friendship are endless and include better health, more relaxed lives and a feeling of unity with the world.

Isn't it time we all got started?

Endnotes

Preface
Page

ix Wolf, Thomas, from **My Other Loneliness: Letters of Thomas Wolf and Aline Bernstein,** Suzanne Stutman, ed., Chapel Hill, NC: Univ. of North Carolina Press, 1983, p. 194.

x   One of my favorite books and most influential is **The Longest War, Sex Differences in Perspective** by Carol Tavris and Carole Offir. This book and **The Mermaid and the Minotaur** by Dorothy Dinnerstein introduced me to the sex differences which act as barriers to equal relationships between men and women.

Chapter 1

1   Pogrebin, p. 35.

3   Cooke, Alistair, **Six Men,** NY: Knopf, 1977, pp. 4-5.

4   Lewis, C.S., **The Four Loves,** NY: Harcourt, Brace, 1960, p. 96.

6   Zilboorg, Gregory, "Loneliness," *Atlantic Monthly,* January 1938, pp. 45-54.

8   Books about friendships between men and women appeared in *The New York Times Book Review*, January 19, 1992, p. 1: **"The Letters of Evelyn Waugh and Diana Cooper,"** ed. by Artemis Cooper, reviewed by William F. Buckley Jr., and **A Woman, A Man, and**

Two Kingdoms, the Story of Madame d'Epinay and the Abbe Galiani, by Francis Steegmuller, reviewed by Victor Bombert. The letter to Madame E'Epinay from Rousseau is found on pages 111-114 in *The Norton Book of Friendship,* ed. by Eudora Welty and Ronald Sharp, NY: W.W. Norton, 1991. The collaboration and friendship between these editors is also worth examining.

8   Brown, Rita Mae, as quoted by Pogrebin, p. 338.

9   Phillips and Goodall, p. 64.

Table 1.1, Miller, Rubin, Pogrebin and Lyon citations are in the bibliography. Drury Sherrod's chapter is in Brod. Keith Davis "Near and Dear: Friendship and Love Compared," *Psychology Today* February 1985, p. 22 et seq.

16   Boland, Susan, cited in *Atlanta Journal/Constitution*, May 29, 1991.

17   McGill, pp. 158, 223.

18   Shaver, Vicki Helgeson, Phillip Shaver & Margeret Dyer "Proto-types of Intimacy and Distance in Same-Sex and Opposite-Sex Relationships," *J. of Social And Personal Relationships*, 4, (1987), pp. 195-233.

18   Remoff, Heather Trexler, **Sexual Choice,** NY: Dutton/Lewis, 1984. Trexler did her research to answer the question why women who said they wanted relationships with sensitive men chose sexual liaisons with "corporate lawyers"? The top three traits associated with male sexual attractiveness were "good-looking, intelligent and good income potential," p. 114.

20   Mount, F., **The Subversive Family,** London: Jonathan Cape, 1983, p. 195. **Blue Highways,** p. 306. Kennedy in Michaelis, p. 125 et seq.

22   Ackroyd story in Michaelis, p. 267 et seq.

24   Nouwen, Henri, quote sent by a friend.

25   Michaelis, p. 211 et seq.

Chapter 2

27   Sandburg, Carl, from Chicago Poems in **The Complete Poems of Carl Sandburg,** NY: Harcort, Brace, Jankovitch.

32   "More than 40 percent . . ." **Singles, The New Americans,** Jacqueline Simenauer and David Carroll, NY: Simon & Schuster, 1982, p. 232.

"About one fifth . . ." Robert Atkinson, "Respectful, Dutiful Teen-agers," *Psychology Today*, Oct. 1988, pp. 22-23.

"Americans in the twenty-five . . ." Marstin E.P. Siligman, "Boomer Blues," *Psychology Today*, Oct. 1988, pp. 55-60.

33 "Loneliness is . . ." Sam Julty, **Men's Bodies, Men's Selves,** NY: Dell, 1979, p. 78.

34 Burton, Robert, **The Anatomy of Melancholy,** NY: Vintage, 1932, p. 245.

34 Lawrence, D.H., **Studies in Classic American Literature,** NY: Thomas Seltzer, 1923, p. 92.

39 Bernikow, Louise, **Alone in America, The Search for Companionship,** NY: Harper & Row, 1986, p. 18.

39 "Recent Surveys . . ." James S. House, Karl R. Landis and Debra Umberson, "Social Relationships and Health," *Science* 241 (1988): pp. 540-545.

39 The studies on the heart patients by Robert B. Case of New York and Dr. Redford B. Williams of Duke University Medical Center were reported in the *Atlanta Journal/Constitution* 1-22-1992, p. E2.

Studies of demoralized men and women by Randy Page and Galen Cole, "Demoralization and living alone: outcomes from an urban community study," *Psychological Reports*, 70, (1992), pp. 275-280.

"Divorced men . . ." **People Need People,** Brent Hafen and Kathryn Frandsen, Evergreen, CO: Cardillera, 1987, p. 27-41.

40 Sadler, William and Johnson, Thomas, Jr., "From Loneliness to Anomia," Chapter 2 in **The Anatomy of Loneliness,** eds. Joseph Hartog, J. Ralph Audy and Yehudi A. Cohen, NY: International Univ. Press, 1980.

44 Ottenberg, Donald, "Initiation of Social Support Systems — A Grass Roots Perspective," in **Stress and Addiction,** Edward Gotheil and others, eds., NY: Brunner/Mazel, 1987, pp. 209-223.

44 Torrence, Gwen, "Torrence: Loneliness a problem for some" by Karen Rosen, *Atlanta Journal/Constitution* 12-22-91, p. E12.

Chapter 3

49 "As one author observed," L. Sprague de Camp quoted in *The New York Times Magazine*, April 7, 1991, p. 38.

53 Chodorow, p. 103.

53 "TV Infants," *Psychology Today*, June 1989, p. 29.

Physiology of Parents in Rete and Field, Ann Frodi, "Variations in Parental and Nonparental Response to Early Communication," pp. 351-356.

54   Blindfolded Mothers reported in *Atlanta Journal/Constitution*, 2-28-1992, p. D2.
Research by Marsha Kaitz in Jan. issue of **Developmental Psychology**.

Tiffeny Field in Rete and Field, "Attachment as Psychobiological Attunement: Being on the Same Wavelength," pp. 415-450.

54   Chodorow, p. 201.

55   Bowlby, John, "Affectional Bonds: Their Nature and Origin" in Weiss, pp. 38-52.

56   Chodorow, pp. 59, 60, 68.

56   Boy's Toilet Training, Constance Perin, **Belonging in America,** p. 175 et seq.

57   Chodorow, pp. 104-105.
Augustus Napier, **The Fragile Bond,** NY: Harper & Row, 1988, p. 307.

57   The Sexual Dichotomy in Chodorow summary of her Chapter 12.

58   Mary Ainsworth, and others, **Patterns of Attachment,** Hillsdale, NJ: Erlbaum, 1978.

58   Shaver, Phillip, and Cindy Hazan, "Being Lonely, Falling in Love: Perspective from Attachment Theory" in Loneliness: Theory, Research, and Applications. [Special issue]. *J. of Social Behavior and Personality*, 2, (1987), pp. 105-124. Beside the Shaver and Hazan reference above, see also Shaver, Hazan and Bradshaw "Love as Attachment" in **The Psychology of Love,** Robert J. Sternberg and Michael L. Barnes Eds., New Haven: Yale University Press, 1988, pp. 69-99.

59   High Risk Infants, see Nathan Fox, "Behavioral and Autonomic Antecedents of Attachment in High-Risk Infants," in Reete and Field, pp. 389-411.

61   Harlow, **From Learning to Love, The Selected Papers Of H.F. Harlow,** Clara Mears Harlow, ed., NY: Prager, 1986, p. 317.

Margolis, p. 262.

62   Adolescent Chimpanzees in "Life and Death at Gombe" by Jane Goodall, *National Geographic*, May 1979, pp. 592-621.

Joseph Campbell, **The Power of Myth,** NY: Doubleday, 1988, p. 81.

63 "Between Five and 15 . . ." "Respectful, Dutiful Teenagers," by Robert Atkinson in *Psychology Today*, October 1988, pp. 22-26. A summary of his book **Teenage World: Adolescent Self-Image in Ten Countries,** Plenum, 1988. Separate study "Loneliness and the Adolescent," Eric Ostrov and Daniel Offer, in Hartog, pp. 170-185; Van Hasselt, Vincent and Michael Hersen, **Handbook of Adolescent Psychology,** NY: Pergamon, 1987.

How we learn friendship is summarized from **Conversations of Friends,** edited by John M. Gottman and Jeffrey G. Parker, NY: Cambridge, 1985.

64 Peer Separation, Field in Rete and Field above "Two therapists," Robert Selman and Lynn Hickey Schultz; Schultz, Norman R, Jr. and DeWayne Moore, "Further Reflections on Loneliness Research; Commentary on Weiss's Assessment of Loneliness Research," 1987, *J. of Social Behavior and Personality*, 2, pp. 37-40.

Lobdell, Judith and Daniel Perlman. "The Intergenerational Transmission of Loneliness: A Study of College Females and Their Parents," *J. Marriage & Family*, 48, 1986, pp. 589-595.

66 McAnarhey, Elizabeth, quoted in **People Need People** by Brent Hafen and Kathryn Frandsen, Evergreen, CO: Cardillera, 1987, pp. 27-41.

66 Learning parenting begins in kindergarten and is taught through grade 6 at the Germantown Friends School. See a description of this in Chapter 6 in **Boys Will Be Boys** by Myriam Miedzian, and Education through Parenting, Philadelphia.

69 Konner, Melvin, **Childhood,** Boston: Little Brown, 1991.

Chapter 4

71 Satir, Virginia, **Peoplemaking,** Palo Alto, CA: Science and Behavior Books, 1972, pp. 30, 79.

75 Sherrod, in Brod, Chapter 9.

76 Tannen, p. 218.

80 Dealing with Conflict, Healey, Jonathan, and Robert Bell, "Assessing Alternative Responses to Conflicts" in **Intimates in Conflict: A Communication Perspective,** Dudley Cahn, ed., 1990, pp. 25-48.

81 Two researchers . . . Ginsberg, Dorthy, and John Gottman, "Conversations of College Roommates: Similarities and Differences in Male and Female Friendship" in Gottman and Parker, **Conver-**

sations of Friends: Speculations On Affective Development, NY: Cambridge, 1986, pp. 290-291.

81 I am indebted to Deborah Tannen's **That's Not What I Mean!** for the framing and metamessage concepts of conversation.

81 Desmond Morris, et al., **Gestures: Their Origins and Distribution,** NY: Stein & Day, 1979, p. xi.

85 Young, Jeffry, "Loneliness, Depression and Cognitive Therapy: Theory and Application" in **Loneliness A Sourcebook of Current Theory, Research and Therapy,** Anne Peplau and Daniel Perlman, eds., NY: John Wiley, 1982, pp. 379-405.

88 Steps To Resolution, Healey and Bell, above.

Chapter 5

93 Konner, Melvin, **The Tangled Wing,** NY: Holt, Rinehart & Winston, 1982.

94 C.R. Carpenter in Holloway, Ralph, **Primate Aggression, Territoriality, and Xenophobia,** NY: Academic Press, 1974, Chapter 10 notes.

94 Ellison, Ralph, **The Invisible Man,** NY: Random House, 1947. **The Masai** from Bandinter, Elizabeth, **Man/Woman, One is the Other,** London: Collins Harvill, 1986, pp. 12-13.

How the sexes relate is modified from Tannen.

98 Phillips and Goodall, p. 108.

98 Ferrigno, "Mysteries of Male Friendship," **Sacramento Bee,** 5-24-1984, "Scene," pp. 1-2.

98 Margaret Thatcher, *Time,* March 12, 1984, p. 67.

99 Block and Greenberg, p. 229.

99 Buss, David, reported in *Atlanta Journal/Constitution,* Aug. 23, 1991, p. D3.

100 Weinberg, George, **Society and the Healthy Homosexual,** NY: St. Martins, 1972, p. 1.

102 Stony, Brook, B. Gladue, R. Green and R. Hellman, "Neuroendocrine Response to Estrogen and Sexual Orientation, *Science,* 255, 1984, pp. 1496-1599.

"Biologic Influences . . ." in Brod.

103 Sissy Boys, Green, Richard, **The "Sissy Boy Syndrome" and the Development of Homosexuality,** New Haven: Yale U. Press, 1987.

Twins, "A Genetic Study of Male Sexual Orientation," J. Michael Bailey and Richard C. Pillard, **Archives of General Psychiatry** 48, 1991, pp. 1089-96. See also "A Difference in Hypothalamic Structure Between Heterosexual and Homosexual Men," Simon LeVay, *Science,* 253, 1991, pp. 1034-37.

103 The list of famous homosexuals is long. I refer you to **Homosexuals in History** by A.L. Rowse, NY: MacMillan, 1977.

105 McGill, Michael, p. 219.

106 Resnick, quoted by Ruthe Stein in **The S. F. Chronicle,** July 20, 1971, p. 152.

Letty Pogrebin, p. 293.

Victoria Vetere quoted by Pogrebin, p. 293.

107 Margolies, p. 85.

107 Jeffres in **Medical Aspects of Human Sexuality,** "Viewpoints: Do men have better relationships with each other than women do with other women?" September 1979, pp. 32-47.

107 Eichenbaume and Orbach, pp. 181-182.

108 Brain, Robert, **Friends and Lovers,** NY: Basic Books, 1976, p. 52.

108 The four Greek loves are modified slightly from Rollo May's **Love and Will,** NY: Norton, 1969, pp. 37-38.

109 Oliner, Pearl and Samuel, **The Altruistic Personality: Rescuers of Jews in Nazi Europe,** NY: Free Press, 1988.

109 Developmental Stages in Friendship: Selman and Schultz and Interdependency "Personal Choice and Social Constraint in Close Relationships: Applications of Network Analysis," Robert Milardo in **Friendship and Social Interaction,** Valerian Derlega and Barbara Winstead, eds., pp. 145-166.

110 Davis, Keith, see Chapter 1, endnotes for Table 1.

110 Kesey, Ken, quoted in *Esquire.*

110 Janet, quoted in Block and Greenberg, p. 102.

111 Rubin p. 159.

112 Farrell, Warren, **Why Men are the Way They Are,** NY: McGraw-Hill, 1986.

Chapter 6

115 Peele, Stanton, **Love Addiction,** NY: New American Library, 1975, p. 56.

117 Endorphins, Rogers and Cooper, eds.

118 Douglas, Kirk, **Ragman's Son,** NY: Simon and Schuster, 1988, p. 113.

118 Mura, David, **A Male Grief: Notes on Pornography and Addiction,** Minneapolis, MN: Milkweed Editions, 1987, p. 21.

119 Zilbergeld, Bernie **Male Sexuality,** NY: Simon and Schuster, 1978, p. 90.

119 Shaver, Phillip, Cindy Hazan and Donna Bradshaw, "Love as Attachment" in **The Psychology of Love,** Robert J. Sternberg and Michael L. Barnes, eds., New Haven: Yale U. Press, 1988, pp. 68-99.

120 Tennov, Dorothy, **Love and Limerence,** Briarcliff Manor, NY: Stein and Day, 1977.

120 Annette Lawson, **Adultery** reviewed in *Psychology Today,* Nov. 1989, p. 65 and in *NY Times Book Review,* Jan. 29, 1989.

120 Barrymore, John, Sarah Bernhardt, Howard Hughes, Byron, Boswell and Rousseau in "Compulsive Sex" **Harvard Magazine** March-April, 1990, pp. 5-6.

121 Dewhurst, Colleen, quoted by Richard Meryman, *Lear's,* Nov/Dec 1988, p. 152.

121 Wilhelm Reich, **Passion of Youth: An Autobiography, 1897-1922,** NY: Farrar, Straus & Giroux.

121 **A Sexual Profile of Men in Power,** Sam Hanus, Barbara Bess, Carol Saltus, NY: Warner Books, 1977.

122 **Lonely All the Time,** Ralph Earle and Gregory Crow with Kevin Osborn, NY: Simon & Schuster, 1989, p. 3.

122 Harvy Jackins, **A Rational Theory of Sexuality,** Seattle, WA: Rational Island Publishers, 1977.

122 Slater, Philip, **Wealth Addiction,** NY: E.P. Dutton, 1980, p. 34.

123 Harry Levinson quoted in "The Entrepreneurial Self," *Psychology Today,* June 1989, pp. 60-63.

123 Shaver and Hazan, "Love and Work, An Attachment-Theoretical Perspective," *J. Personality and Social Psychology,* 59, 1990, pp. 270-280.

124 Margaret A. Shotton, **Computer Addiction: A Study of Computer Dependency,** NY: Taylor & Francis, 1989, p. 261.

124 Slater, above.

124 Friedman, Meyer, quoted by Tony Schwartz, "The Acceleration Syndrome," *Vanity Fair*, October 1988, p. 144.

124 Adrenaline Adventures, Colorado described by Bob Garfield on Public Radio, *All Things Considered*, August 27, 1991.

125 Gambling, cover story in *Time*, July 10, 1989, pp. 16-21.

Dorthy Meyer Gaev, **The Psychology of Loneliness,** Chicago: Adams, 1976, p. 35.

125 Brody, Jane, column in *Atlanta Journal/Constitution*, Aug. 22, 1991, p. E11.

Levinthal, p. 15.

126 Carolyn Wesson, quoted in *The Atlanta Journal/Constitution*, March 12, 1990, p. B3.

126 Shoplifting, *Psychology Today*, November 1988, p. 10.

Christina's Story reported by Steven Beeber in **Creative Loafing,** December 10, 1988, p. 19A.

127 Moon, Heat, **Blue Highways,** p. 237.

127 Jack Katz, **Seductions of Crime,** NY: Basic, 1989.

128 475 Million Pets, **In the Company of Animals** by James Serpell, reported in *Time*, August 18, 1986, p. 71.

128 Therapeutic Pets by Robin Marantz Henig in *AARP News Bulletin*, December 1988, p. 2.

128 Lewis Grizzard in *Atlanta Journal/Constitution*, April 8, 1990, p. D1.

130 Endorphins and Alcohol. Levinthal, p. 155.

131 Peele, Stanton, **Diseasing of America,** Lexington, MA: D.C. Heath, 1989; see also Fingarette, Herbert, **Heavy Drinking: The Myth of Alcoholism as a Disease,** Berkeley: U. Calif. Press, 1988.

132 Dopamine Metabolism and Alcoholism — "New Studies Lend Support to 'Alcoholism Gene' Finding" by Michael Waldholz, *The Wall Street Journal*, Monday, July 15, 1981, p. B1.

133 Bill Wilson quote in **Not God, A History of Alcoholics Anonymous** by Ernest Kurtz, Center City, MN: Hazelden, 1979, p. 205.

133 Carnes, Patrick, **Out of The Shadows: Understanding Sexual Addiction.**

135 Schaeffer, James, in *Psychology Today*, March 1989.

135 Hank Williams, **Sing a Sad Song, The Life of Hank Williams** by Roger Williams, Garden City, NY: Doubleday, 1970.

135 Barrymore, Drew, reported in *Atlanta Journal/Constitution*, Feb. 14, 1990, p. F10.

136 Lucy Barry Robe, **Co-starring Famous Women and Alcohol,** Minneapolis, MN: CompCare, 1986.

137 Milkman and Sunderwirth, **Craving for Ecstasy,** Lexington, MA: Lexington, 1987, p. 28.

138 Graham, Kathryn, "Reasons for Consumption and Heavy Caffeine Use: Generalization of a Model Based on Alcohol Research," *Addictive Behaviors*, 13, 1989, pp. 209-214.

138 Teen Cocaine Use, Maddahian, E., "Adolescent Drug Use And Intention to use Drugs: Concurrent and Longitudinal Analysis of Four Ethnic Groups," *Addictive Behaviors*, 13, 1988, pp. 191-195.

140 Hollis, Judi, **Fat is a Family Affair** Center City, MN: Hazelden, 1985, p. xii.

141 Neill, Darryl, quoted by Susan Percy in "If It Feels Good . . ." *Atlanta Magazine*, Nov. 1988, pp. 83-85.

142 **The Paleolithic Prescription,** S. Boyd Eaton, Marjorie Shostak and Melvin Konner, NY: Harper & Row, 1988.

143 Obesity, see John S. Daniels "Obesity" in *Eating Disorders*, Felix, E.F. and Larocca, D., San Francisco: Jossey-Bass, 1986, pp. 47-59

143 Mainland Chinese, Cornell University Press reported in *Atlanta Journal/Constitution*, May 8, 1990, p. F1.

144 **The Etiology and Treatment of Bulimia Nervosa,** Craig Johnson & Mary Connors, NY: Basic, 1987.

144 Brumberg, John Jacobs, **Fasting Girls: The Emergence of Anorexia Nervosa as a Modern Disease,** Cambridge, MA: Harvard Univ. Press, 1988.

145 Maine, Margo

145 Dana, Mira, "Boundaries: One-Way Mirror to the Self" in **Fed Up and Hungry,** Marilyn Lawrence, ed., NY: Peter Bedrick, 1987, pp. 46-60.

146 "The Endogenous Opioid Peptides: Relationship to Food Intake, Obesity, and Sweet Tastes" by Robin Marks-Kaufman and Robin B. Kanarek in **Eating Behavior in Eating Disorders,** B. Timothy Walsh, ed., Washington: American Psychiatric Press, 1988.

147 Winfrey, Oprah, quoted in *Essence,* June 1989, p. 46.

Chapter 7

149 Miller, Stuart, p. 195.

152 Lindbergh, Ann Morrow, **A Gift from the Sea,** NY: Random House, 1955.

153 Thoreau, Henry, **Walden and Other Writings,** NY: Bantam, 1962, p. 172.

155 Thoreau, p. 343.

155 Ecclesiastes, **The New English Bible,** Cambridge: Cambridge U. Press, 1971.

155 Abbey, Edward, **Desert Solitaire,** NY: Ballantine, 1968, p. 216.

155 Sarton, May, **Journal of a Solitude,** NY: Norton, 1973.

157 Storr, Anthony, **Solitude,** NY: Free Press, 1988.

Chapter 8

164 Shostak, Margorie, personal communication and **Nisa: The Life and Words of a !Kung Women,** NY: Vintage, 1983.

164 Lee, Richard, **The !Kung San: Men Women and Work in a Foraging Society,** Boston: Cambridge U. Press, 1979.

Friendly Bonding, Irenaus-Eibesfeld, "The Myth of the Aggression Free Hunter and Gatherer Society" In Holloway, pp. 455-456, see Chapter 6.

Hxaro is described by Polly Wessner in Leacock, Eleanor and Richard Lee, **Politics and History in Band Societies.** NY: Cambridge U. Press, 1982.

165 Silberbauer, George, **Hunter and Habitat in the Central Kalahari Desert,** NY: Cambridge U. Press, 1982.

165 Mbuti, see Turnbull and Turnbull in Lee, Richard and Irven Devore, **Man the Hunter,** Chicago: Aldine, 1968.

166 The Gilgamesh story, written as early as 2000 B.C., contains a deluge myth and several visits to hell. See Vincent Kavaloski,

"Men and the Dream of Brotherhood" in Robert Lewis, **Men in Difficult Times,** Englewood Cliffs, NY: Prentice-Hall, 1981. pp. 199-212. Less known is the theme that Gilgamesh assists his sister, Inanna, to claim rulership of Urak. This begins the legend of "mighty, majestic, radiant and ever youthful" queens. See D. Wolkstein and S.N. Kramer, **Inanna, Queen of Heaven and Earth: Her Stories and Hymns from Summer,** NY: Harper & Row, 1983.

For many of the classic friendships, see **Eros: An Anthology of Friendship,** Alistair Sutherland and Patrick Anderson, eds., NY: Arno Press, 1961, 1975.

170 Nin, Anais, "D. H. Lawrence: An Unprofessional Study," in the **Anais Nin Reader,** Philip Jason, ed., NY: Criterion Books, 1960.

171 London, Jack, letter in **American Dreamers, Charmian and Jack London,** by Clarice Staz, NY: St. Martin's Press, 1988.

171 Tiger, Lionel, **Men in Groups,** NY: Random House, 1969: Marion Boyars, 1984.

171 Fraternal organizations from **The Secret Societies of all Ages and Countries,** Charles Heckethorn, University Books, 1965.

173 Bohemian Club — Report on NPR, August 30, 1982. Worker interviewed described some men as "drunk all the time" and men dancing dressed as women. See also G. William Domhoff, **The Bohemian Grove and Other Retreats,** NY: Harper & Row, 1974; and Thomas Gregor, "No Girls Allowed," in *Science, 82,* December, pp. 27-31.

174 Daniell, Rosemary, **Fatal Flowers,** NY: Holt, Rinehart and Winston, 1980, p. 166.

Florence King, **Southern Ladies and Gentlemen,** NY: Stein & Day, 1975, Chapter 6.

174 Le Masters, E.E., **Blue Collar Aristocrats,** Madison: U. of Wisconsin, 1975.

175 Steinmann, Anne and David Fox, **The Male Dilemma,** NY: Jason Aronson, 1974, p. 97.

Harold Lyon, p. 182, see Chapter 2.

175 Carol the Stripper, quoted in **Ponce de Leon** by George Mitchell, Atlanta: Argonne Books, 1983.

176 Red Men in Mark C. Carnes, **Secret Ritual and Manhood in Victorian America,** New Haven: Yale U. Press, 1989.

176 Dyer, Gwynne, **War,** NY: Crown, 1985, p. 104.

177 Philip Caputo, **A Rumor of War,** NY: Holt, Reinhart & Winston, 1987, p. xvii.

177 Broyles, William, Jr., **Brothers in Arms,** NY: Avon, 1986.

Chapter 9

187 Burnett, Carol, and Julie Andrews, "She's My Best Friend," by Ellen Hawkes, *Parade Magazine*, Dec. 3, 1989, p. 5.

188 Lerner, Gerda, **The Creation of Patriarchy,** NY: Oxford U. Press, 1986, p. 31.

188 Cott, Nancy, **The Bonds of Womanhood,** New Haven: Yale U. Press., 1977.

188 Quaker Friends, Margaret Hope Bacon, **Mothers of Feminism,** NY: Harper & Row, 1986.

189 Women's organizations in *New York Times Book Review*, May 17, 1992, of **"Natural Allies, Women's Associations in American History"** by Anne Fior Scott (Urbana: U. of Illinois Press) review by Laurel Thatcher Ulrich, p. 11.

189 Carol Smith-Rosenberg quoted by Sherrod in Brod p. 233.

190 Teri Apter, **Altered Loves, Mothers and Daughters During Adolescence,** NY: St. Martin's Press, 1990.

191 One novelist Carol Shields, **Swann,** NY: Viking.

191 Judith P. Salzman, "Save the World, Save Myself: Responses to Problematic Attachment," in **Making Connections: The Relational Worlds of Adolescent Girls at Emma Willard School,** Carol Gilligan, Nona Lyons and Trudy Hanmer, eds., Troy, NY: Emma Willard School, 1989.

192 Judith Briles, **Women to Woman: From Sabotage to Support,** NY: New Horizon Press.

192 Tara Roth Madden, **Women Versus Women: The Uncivil Business War,** NY: Amacom.

192 "Only 2.6 Percent of U.S. Corporate Officers Are Women, Study Says," *Atlanta Journal/Constitution*, Aug. 26, 1991, p. 33.

193 Margolies, p. 9.

Chapter 10

197 Alberoni, Francesco, **L'Amitie,'** France, Ramsay, 1985, quoted by Elizabeth Badinter in **Man/Woman, One is the Other,** London: Collins Harvill, 1986, p. 207.

199 "Equal Treatment of Women" — Badinter considers male dominance has been on its last legs since Louis XVI lost his head, pp. 56-57.

200 "Love, lies, and fear in the plague years . . .," by Simon Sebag Montefiore, *Psychology Today*, Sept/Oct, 1992, pp. 30-35.

202 "One Survey," *Psychology Today*, Sept/Oct, 1992, p. 12.

202 Prather, Hugh. **Notes to Myself,** NY: Bantam, 1987.

204 Couples Communication: there are many books outlining communication techniques. One I have found helpful is Harville Hendrix's **Getting the Love You Want.**

204 L'Engle, Madeleine, **Two Part Invention,** NY: Farrar, Straus & Giroux, 1988.

205 Working colleagues and courtship, **More Than Friends, Less Than Lovers,** David R. Eyler and Andrea P. Baridon, Los Angeles: Tarcher, 1990.

206 Chassier in *Ms* August, 1984, p. 51.

208 Men's and Women's support groups: I have found Bill Kauth's, **A Circle of Men,** to be helpful in forming groups, New York: St. Martins, 1992.

209 12-Step resources in Appendix 2.

211 Bradshaw, John, **Healing the Shame That Binds You,** Deerfield Beach, FL: Health Communications, 1988, p. 7. This book will help most in recognizing and dealing with the shame. Some will find therapeutic help necessary.

211 **Clearness: Processes for Supporting Individuals & Groups In Decision-Making,** Peter Woodrow, Philadelphia: New Society Publishers, 1983.

213 The questions came from reading Carla Wills-Brandon, **Learning To Say No: Establishing Healthy Boundaries,** Deerfield Beach, FL: Health Communications, 1990. Helps examine these questions.

214 Bender, Sue, **Plain and Simple,** San Francisco: Harper, 1991, p. 123.

216 "Meeting in the Middle," Patti Davis writing in *Esquire*, October, 1991 pp. 149-50, "We're still on opposite sides of the room at a school dance, wondering who should make the first move. We could just meet in the middle of the floor, but that would be too easy — or too difficult. We've grown too comfortable with our own sides of the room."

Chapter 11

221 Leake, Chauncy, **What Are We Living For?** Westbury, NY: PJD Publications Ltd., 1973, p. 173.

Storr, See Chapter 7.

Bibliography

Block, Joel and Diane Greenberg, *Women and Friendship*, NY: Franklin Watts, 1985.

Brain, Robert, *Friends and Lovers*, NY: Basic Books, 1976.

Brod, Harry, *The Making of Masculinities*, Boston: Allen & Unwin, 1987.

Chodorow, Nancy, *The Reproduction of Mothering*, Berkeley, CA: University of California Press, 1978.

Eichenbaum, Luise and Susie Orbach, *Between Women*, NY: Viking Penguin, 1987.

Leefeldt, Christine and Ernest Callenbach, *The Art of Friendship*, NY: Berkley, 1979.

Levinthal, Charles, *Messengers of Paradise, Opiates and the Brain*, NY: Doubleday, 1988.

Lyon, Harold C., *Tenderness is Strength, From Machismo to Manhood*, NY: Harper & Row, 1977.

Margolis, Eve, *The Best of Friends, The Worst of Enemies*, Garden City, NY: Doubleday, 1987.

McGill, Michael, *The McGill Report on Male Intimacy*, NY: Holt, Rinehart, Winston, 1984.

Michaelis, David, *The Best of Friends: Profiles of Extraordinary Friendships*, NY: Morrow, 1983.

Miller, Stuart, *Men and Friendship*, Boston: Houghton Mifflin, 1983.

Perin, Constance, *Belonging in America, Reading Between the Lines*, Madison, WI: University Wisconsin Press, 1988.

Phillips, Gerald M. and H. Lloyd Goodall, *Loving and Living, Improve Your Friendships and Marriage*, Englewood Cliffs: Prentice-Hall, 1983.

Pogrebin, Letty, *Among Friends*, NY: McGraw-Hill, 1987.

Rete, Martin, and Tiffany Field, eds., *The Psychobiology of Attachment and Separation*, New York: Academic Press, 1985.

Rodgers, R.J., and S.J. Cooper, eds., *Endorphins, Opiates and Behavioral Processes*, NY: John Wiley, 1988.

Rubin, Lillian, *Just Friends, the Role of Friendship in Our Lives*, NY: Harper & Row, 1985.

Selman, Robert, and Lynn Hickey Schultz, *Making a Friend in Youth*, Chicago: University Chicago Press, 1990.

Tannen, Deborah, *You Just Don't Understand*, NY: William Morrow, 1990.

Weiss, Richard, *Loneliness: The Experience of Emotional and Social Isolation*, Cambridge, MA: MIT Press.

Appendix A

Loneliness Questionnaire

Loneliness has been defined briefly as a state of being alone when you don't want to be alone. It is natural to feel lonely; we all do at some times. These questions explore that loneliness.

1. How do you feel the following words relate to loneliness? On a scale of 1 to 7 with 1 being the least related, 4 average and 7 most. Please rate these words:

_____	1. desperate	_____	15. anxiety
_____	2. hopeless	_____	16. desolated
_____	3. painful	_____	17. cheerful
_____	4. shyness	_____	18. isolated
_____	5. depressing	_____	19. meaningless
_____	6. liberating	_____	20. uncontrollable
_____	7. detached	_____	21. angry
_____	8. hopeful	_____	22. worthless
_____	9. powerless	_____	23. opportunity
_____	10. emptiness	_____	24. unattached
_____	11. failure	_____	25. exciting
_____	12. workaholism	_____	26. obsessive
_____	13. individualism	_____	27. _____
_____	14. alone	_____	28. _____

2. Is being alone and being lonely different? How are they the
same or different?

_____

_____

_____

_____

3. When are you likely to feel lonely? Please check those that
apply to you.

_____ At work?   _____ On the weekend?

_____ After work?   _____ In a group of people?

_____ In the evening?   _____ With a spouse or

_____ Late at night?   significant partner?

4. When have you been most lonely? Describe the situation(s).

_____

_____

_____

_____

5. How do you deal with your loneliness?

_____

_____

_____

_____

6. Have you ever done the following when you felt lonely? *Rank*
as many as apply by 1 = most frequently to 10 = least frequently.

_____ Ate a lot?   _____ Sought sex or

_____ Drank a lot of alcohol?   pornography?

_____ Watched more TV   _____ Exercised?
         than usual?
                                   _____ Read a lot?
_____ Worked longer than
         usual?   _____ Went shopping?

_____ Used drugs?   _____ Sought the company
                                            of others?

7. How often do you feel lonely, check one?

_____ A few times a year   _____ Nearly every day

_____ Once or twice a month _____ Daily

_____ Once or twice a week

8. Indicate how often you feel the way described in each of the following statements. *Circle* one number for each.

	Never	Rarely	Sometimes	Often
A. I feel in tune with the people around me.	1	2	3	4
B. No one really knows me well.	1	2	3	4
C. I can find companionship when I want it.	1	2	3	4
D. People are around me but not with me.	1	2	3	4

9. How would you rate your relationship with your mother on a scale of 1 to 7, 1 being very little intimacy?

_____ As a child   _____ As a young adult
_____ As an adolescent   _____ Now

10. How would you rate your relationship with your father on a scale of 1 to 7, 1 being very little intimacy?

_____ As a child   _____ As a young adult
_____ As an adolescent   _____ Now

11. How would you rate your relationship with your peer group on a scale of 1 to 7, 1 being very few friendships?

_____ As a child   _____ As a young adult
_____ As an adolescent   _____ Now

12. What do you want from a friendship?

_____

_____

_____

_____

13. What do you have to offer your friends?

_____

_____

_____

_____

14. What advice would you give to someone else who is lonely and wants to know how to meet friends?

_____

_____

_____

_____

Appendix B

Resources

Support Groups (12-Step And Other)

Look for local groups in the White Pages of your phone book.

Adult Children of Alcoholics
Central Service Board
2225 Sepulveda Blvd., #200
Torrance, CA 90505

Alateen Family Groups
Al-Anon Family Service
 Group Headquarters
P.O. Box 862 Midtown Station
New York, NY 10018-0862

Alcoholics Anonymous
468 Park Ave. South
New York, NY 10016

Co-Counseling
 Rational Island Publishers
P.O. Box 2081, Main Office Station
Seattle, WA 98111

Co-Dependents Anonymous
P.O. Box 33577
Phoenix, AZ 85067-3577

Overeaters Anonymous
4025 Spencer St., #3
Torrance, CA 90503

Sex Addicts Anonymous
P.O. Box 3038
Minneapolis, MN 55403

Services

ASPCA
441 E. 92nd St.
New York, NY 10128

American Cancer Society
90 Park Ave.
New York, NY 10017

American Civil Liberties Union
132 W. 43rd St.
New York, NY 10036

American Red Cross
17th & D Streets N.W.
Washington, DC 20006

American Youth Hostels
P.O. Box 37613
Washington, DC 20013

**Americans For Human Rights
and Social Justice**
P.O. Box 6258
Fort Worth, TX 76115

Amnesty International U.S.A.
322 Eighth Ave.
New York, NY 10001

Bread for the World
802 Rhode Island Ave. N.E.
Washington, DC 20018

Common Cause
2030 M St.
Washington, DC 20036

Humane Society of the U.S.
2100 L St. N.W.
Washington DC 20037

Literacy Volunteers of America
5795 Widewaters Parkway
Syracuse, NY 13210

NAACP
4805 Mt. Hope Drive
Baltimore, MD 21215

**National Conference of
   Christians and Jews**
71 Fifth Ave.
New York, NY 10003

National Urban League
500 E. 62nd St.
New York, NY 10020

U.S. Committee for UNICEF
331 E. 38th St.
New York, NY 10016

**United Nations Association
   of the U.S.A.**
485 Fifth Ave.
New York, NY 10017

**Women's International League
   for Peace & Freedom**
1213 Race St.
Philadelphia, PA 19107

YMCA
101 N. Wacker Drive
Chicago, IL 60606

YWCA
726 Broadway
New York, NY 10003

Clubs, Classes And Happenings

Listings can be found in your local newspaper.

Book Signings
Dance Classes (Western, Cajun,
    English Contra, Western
    Square, Ballroom, Tap, Ballet)
Choruses and Orchestras
Exercise Classes and Groups
Fairs, Local Celebrations and
    Carnivals
Film Series and Film Clubs
Foreign Language

Fund Raisers
Gallery Openings
Local Tours of Historic Sites

**National University Extension
    Association**
One Dupont Circle
Suite 360 N.W.
Washington, DC 20036

Volunteers Or Memberships

American Mensa
2626 E. 14th St.
Brooklyn, NY 11235

Crafts

Genealogy

Museums and Libraries

Peace Corps
1990 K. St. N.W.
Washington, DC 20526

Environmental

American Birding Association
618 Lavaca
Austin, TX 78701

Audubon Society
950 3rd Ave.
New York, NY 10022

Friends of the Earth
530 7th St. S.E.
Washington, DC 20003

National Wildlife Federation
1412 16th St. N.W.
Washington, DC 20036

Sierra Club
730 Polk St.
San Francisco, CA 94109

Wilderness Society
900 17th St. N.W.
Washington, DC 20006

Interest Groups And Hobbies

AARP
For Retired People
1909 K St. N.W.
Washington, DC 20049

American Atheists
P.O. Box 140195
Austin, TX 78714

The American Legion
700 N. Pennsylvania
Indianapolis, IN 46204

**Antique Automobile Club
  of America**
501 W. Governor Road
Hershey, PA 17033

National Archery Association
1750 E. Boulder St.
Colorado Springs, CO 80909

**Universal Autograph
  Collectors Club**
P.O. Box 6181
Washington, DC 20044-6181

Bald-Headed Men of America
1 Bald Drive
Morehead City, NC 28557-1466

**Society for Preservation
  Of Barbershop Quartet
  Singing in America**
6315 Third Ave.
Kenosha, WI 53140-5199

**Big Brothers/Big Sisters
  of America**
230 N. 13th St.
Philadelphia, PA 19107

B'nai B'rith International
1640 Rhode Island Ave. N.W.
Washington, DC 20036

**Campers & Hikers
  Association, Inc.**
7172 Transit Road
Buffalo, NY 14221

Amateur Chamber Music Players
545 Eighth Ave.
New York, NY 10018

Chess League of America
P.O. Box 416
Warrensville, IL 60555

**Circus Fans Association
  of America**
P.O. Box 3187
Flint, MI 48502

**American Contract Bridge
  League**
2200 Democrat Road
Memphis, TN 38116

A Course in Miracles
(Information and book)
N.W. Center for ACIM
Box 1362
Hanlei, HI 96714

**Benevolent and Protective
  Order of Elks of the U.S.A.**
2750 N. Lake View Ave.
Chicago, IL 60630

**Experiment in International
  Living**
P.O. Box 676, Kipling Road
Brattleboro, VT 05302

Foundation for Inner Peace
P.O. Box 635
Tiburon, CA 94920

Garden Club of America
598 Madison Ave.
New York, NY 10022

**National Gay and Lesbian
  Task Force**
1734 14th St. N.W.
Washington, DC 20009

**Gray Panthers
  Consciousness Raising Group
  of Older Adults**
1424 16th St. N.W., Suite 602
Washington, DC 20036

**Hadassah
  The Women's Zionist
  Organization of America**
50 W. 58th St.
New York, NY 10019

U.S. Handball Association
930 N. Benton Ave.
Tucson, AZ 85711

**Mended Hearts
  Heart Disease
  Patients and Friends**
7320 Greenville Ave.
Dallas, TX 75231

U.S. Jaycees
4 West 21st St.
Tulsa, OK 74114

Lefthanders International
P.O. Box 8249
Topeka, KS 66608

**Amateur Magicians Association
  Worldwide**
325 Maple St.
Lynn, MA 01904-0073

**Ninety-Nines
  International Organization
  of Women Pilots**
P.O. Box 59965
Will Rogers Airport
Oklahoma City, OK 73159

Parents Without Partners
8807 Colesville R.
Silver Spring, MD 20910

Poetry Society of America
15 Gramercy Park
New York, NY 10003

Feminist Alliance Against Rape
P.O. Box 21033
Washington, DC 20009

**National Retired Teachers
  Association**
1909 K St. N.W.
Washington, DC 20049

Society of Rosicrucians
321 W. 101st St.
New York, NY 10025

Rotary International
One Rotary Center
Evanson, IL 60201

**Shakespeare Association
  of America**
Dept. of English
SMU
Dallas, TX 75275

Spiritual Emergence Network
250 Grove Ave.
Menlo Park, CA 94025

Tattoo Club of America
822 Ave. of the Americas
New York, NY 10001

American Theatre Organ Society
P.O. Box 343
Olivenhain, CA 92024

Thoreau Society
156 Belknap St.
Concord, MA 01742

Toastmasters International
23182 Arroyo Vista
Rancho Santa Margarita,
   CA 92688

**International
   Toastmistress Clubs**
2519 Woodland Drive
Anaheim, CA 92801

**American Translators
   Association**
109 Croton Ave.
Ossining, NY 10562

International Wizard of Oz Club
P.O. Box 95
Kinderhook, IL 62345

American Watercolor Society
47 Fifth Ave.
New York, NY 10003

**National Organization
   for Women**
1000 16th St. N.W.
   Suite 700
Washington, DC 20036

World Future Society
4916 St. Elmo Ave.
Bethesda, MD 20814

Other Books By . . .
Health Communications

ADULT CHILDREN OF ALCOHOLICS (Expanded)
Janet Woititz

Over a year on *The New York Times* Best-Seller list, this book is the primer on Adult Children of Alcoholics.

ISBN 1-55874-112-7   **$8.95**

STRUGGLE FOR INTIMACY
Janet Woititz

Another best-seller, this book gives insightful advice on learning to love more fully.

ISBN 0-932194-25-7   **$6.95**

BRADSHAW ON: THE FAMILY: A Revolutionary Way of Self-Discovery
John Bradshaw

The host of the nationally televised series of the same name shows us how families can be healed and individuals can realize full potential.

ISBN 0-932194-54-0   **$9.95**

HEALING THE SHAME THAT BINDS YOU
John Bradshaw

This important book shows how toxic shame is the core problem in our compulsions and offers new techniques of recovery vital to all of us.

ISBN 0-932194-86-9   **$9.95**

HEALING THE CHILD WITHIN: Discovery and Recovery for
Adult Children of Dysfunctional Families — Charles Whitfield, M.D.

Dr. Whitfield defines, describes and discovers how we can reach our Child Within to heal and nurture our woundedness.

ISBN 0-932194-40-0   **$8.95**

A GIFT TO MYSELF: A Personal Guide To Healing My Child Within
Charles L. Whitfield, M.D.

Dr. Whitfield provides practical guidelines and methods to work through the pain and confusion of being an Adult Child of a dysfunctional family.

ISBN 1-55874-042-2   **$11.95**

HEALING TOGETHER: A Guide To Intimacy And Recovery For
Co-dependent Couples — Wayne Kritsberg, M.A.

This is a practical book that tells the reader why he or she gets into dysfunctional and painful relationships, and then gives a concrete course of action on how to move the relationship toward health.

ISBN 1-55784-053-8   **$8.95**

3201 S.W. 15th Street,
Deerfield Beach, FL 33442-8190
1-800-441-5569

Health
Communications, Inc.®

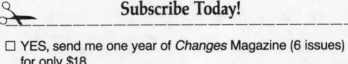